Was That Really Me?

by

Ernest Millington

Fultus™ Books

Was That Really Me?

by

Ernest Millington

Edited by Caro Millington

ISBN 1-59682-076-4

Published by Fultus Corporation

Corporate Web Site: *http://www.fultus.com*
Fultus eLibrary: *http://elibrary.fultus.com*
Online Book Superstore: *http://store.fultus.com*
Writer Web Site *http://writers.fultus.com/millington/*

Contents

Illustrations

Preface

I was a 16-year old school leaver….

… which made me rather privileged as the school leaving age in 1932 was fourteen. I did not feel educationally underprivileged. I had reached the 6th form with three passes in the Higher Schools Certificate – Greek, Latin and French – for which I have always been grateful, and to which I owe my fascination with words, their meanings and origins, and the way in which they can come together in grammatical and syntactical form.

However, what was not so privileged was that I was obliged to leave school as I was expelled from my home by my father at sixteen. I found myself with one suit of clothes, without other possessions of any sort, and the sum of half-a-crown[1] which my elder brother gave me as I left the family home, "to help keep the devil out".

I was already taking an active part in youth politics, and was canvassing and addressing meetings for candidates for a forthcoming local government election. At one house the householder, a Mr George Bond, said: "I am not concerned about politics. What I want to know is how a lad in your circumstances can survive?". When I told him that in effect I was homeless and jobless and, quite honestly, did not know how to go about finding a job, he gave me an address in the City and told me to present myself there at 10 o'clock the following Monday morning. It was the office of William Whiteley, a distiller and blender of whisky, who was in continuous dispute with the more famous Bayswater store of the same name. The following Monday I duly turned up and was interviewed by a Mr Dixon, Chief Accountant to the group of companies headed by William Whiteley. He appointed me clerk and trainee accountant, to start immediately.

I was able to rent a room for 18s 6d a week, and do something about my appearance, as well as being able to eat occasionally. I settled in

---

[1] Twelve and a half pence

very well, and confined my politicking to weekends. One Saturday I was addressing a large and enthusiastic rally in Hyde Park. The following Monday when he arrived in the general office, Mr Whiteley went round, peering in cupboards, emptying wastepaper baskets and apparently searching hard for something lost. When asked what he was looking for, he replied: "There is a Bolshie in the office!"

He had been strolling in the Park on Saturday, and had seen and listened to me addressing the multitude. I was sacked forthwith, and thus began three years of various employment which included beating moths' eggs out of furs, and carrying parcels and messages all over London from head offices to the branches of various enterprises.

I kept up both my political and educational activities. I was secretary of the Far East London region of the Labour Party League of Youth, and a member of its National Advisory Committee. We were not permitted to be on the executive committee, all policy making was the sole prerogative of our parent body. I continued to go to evening classes in Accountancy, partly to help me earn a living, and partly to help in my analysis of the wicked capitalist system. The lowest level of qualification in the accountancy world was awarded by the then Institute of Cost and Works Accountants. I have forgotten the precise name of the certificate, but I was awarded one in 1938.

Ilford had a very flourishing branch of the Workers Education Association. The Chairman was a Ph.D and headmaster, and almost all the members were graduates and employed, usually in a professional capacity. I joined the Economics class, under Dr Monica Felton, whose leadership suited me as she was a Marxist who was later awarded the Stalin Peace Prize. Part of my political development was a growing concern about the growth of Nazism in Germany, and the betrayal of any hopes of future peace by the appeasement policy of Neville Chamberlain. So I joined the Territorial Army to learn how to play a small part in the war which, after the Munich agreement of 1938, seemed inevitable.

My other main interest, inevitably, was emotional. The W.E.A. had a weekly forum. Each member took his turn to read a paper which was then discussed. We met in the drawing rooms of our more affluent members – bigger drawing rooms. There I met Gwen. At 20, with her vivid blue eyes and black wavy hair, she was very beautiful. On our Sunday W.E.A. walks we two tended to walk together. We were in a minority of those who had not been, and had no hope of going, to University. We were the youngest, and tended to be together on these walks. I was invited to tea on Sundays, and there met her mother. Mrs

Olive was a weird woman. She had been married twice, in each case pregnant after a brief holiday romance. Her first husband was a high level trainee of an overseas bank.[2] The rules of his employment forbade marriage before the age of 30, and then only with management permission. He must have been a gent. They got married. He immediately volunteered for military service, although exempt from call-up by virtue of his profession. Gwen was both the cause and the product of this alliance. She was born early in 1914, and her father killed in the trenches at Passchendaele in 1917. His widow, Mrs Pickard, was on holiday by the seaside a few years after the war, where she met and became pregnant by a bachelor schoolmaster who, by coincidence, must at that time have been teaching me. Soon after the birth of his son, quickly followed by that of a daughter, the schoolmaster caught an infection (believed to be meningitis) at the local swimming baths, and died.

So I was introduced to the household of the mother, who had a desperate desire that her daughter should not somehow fall into the trap of an enforced and almost loveless marriage. I confess my attraction to Gwen was very strong, but I was startled to discover that mother and daughter, without discussion with me, had fixed a date for my wedding. I was not yet 21 and so the planners fixed on the Easter weekend after my 21st birthday, as they knew that my father would not give his permission.

There I was, a 21 year old minor clerk, with little or no prospects, married to a young woman two years my senior, who had an exalted sense of her own worth, and an ingrained sense that it was a husband's duty to keep her in the manner she desired. She also had an enormous sense that she had somehow been tricked by fate in that most of her friends were either graduates or qualified teachers.

Then came the Munich crisis. Chamberlain with his piece of paper; the certainty of a war against Germany, and being trapped in the Territorial Army. In July 1939 we went into camp as part of the Air Defence of Great Britain. By September we had not been allowed home except for a day or so since July, and in September we were fully mobilised.

The unit of which I was a humble member consisted of ten men. The sergeant in charge was a regular soldier. His deputy, a corporal, had

---

[2] The Chartered Bank of Hong Kong

been in the Territorial Army for years. The other eight were better educated, except in the arts of war, than the N.C.O.s, and were all recommended for commissions. I went to Shrivenham, the Royal Artillery Officer Training Unit, and discovered that the rapid expansion of the Army was calling for the equally rapid training and promotion of young officers to fill the many gaps which conscription had created. The first few months of the war were a period of incredible boredom. During the day we sought to make soldiers of a body of conscripts, drawn mainly from the East End of London, who gave a whole new meaning to the word 'non-cooperative'. Then, at the end of 1939, the Army Council advertised for young officers with appropriate education and health qualifications, to apply to learn to fly. If they were successful in obtaining their wings, then they were immediately transferred and posted to units from where they were made ready to serve in one of the Commands of the R.A.F.

Possibly because by this time I was a young father I was selected for Flying Training Command (almost all the ex-Army transferees wanted to be fighter boys). I went to Montrose and duly qualified as a pilot-instructor, a job I still consider to have been more dangerous than flying on active operations. There I learnt that with concentration I could become a very good pilot. As with all teaching, an important part of the job is demonstration. With flying, training demonstration not carried out to a fairly high standard could be fatal – for the students when they were sent solo.

The average age of the young men training as pilots in the wartime R.A.F. was, at this time, about 20. Consequently an elderly gent like me, married and a father, and with commissioned experience in the Army, was ripe for promotion. I rapidly became a Flight Lieutenant and was posted for heavy bomber training. I served a little time in 49 Squadron, and then went off to 44 Squadron where I was senior Flight Lieutenant. Each of the two flights was commanded by a Squadron Leader. The Commanding Officer, a Rhodesian Wing Commander, had completed his tour of operations and was awaiting posting. One dreadful night there were very heavy losses, including both of 44 Squadron Flight Commanders. I woke up to find that I was the senior officer and therefore acting as C.O., the job of a Wing Commander.

The next day all squadron commanders and above had been summoned to a 5 Group conference on daylight bombing. I checked with H.Q. and was told that as senior officer, although only a Flight Lieutenant, I had to attend. In the morning the Senior Air Staff Officer set out the tactics which would come into force immediately for daylight attacks over enemy territory. This was based upon the Squadrons flying in formation, as the Americans were doing in their Fortresses, and being led by a master crew who would be responsible for finding the target. S.A.S.O. was a convincing talker, and most of the audience were ambitious, so there was a high degree of agreement. Eventually I couldn't stand what I conceived of as the nonsense being talked. So, in spite of my junior status, I intervened and condemned the whole plan as impossible. My condemnation was based on the fact that pilots with no training in formation flying (except a few hours on very light training aircraft such as the Tiger Moth) were expected to be able to take four-engined Lancasters with a full bomb and fuel load into a difficult manoeuvre which American pilots had spent months learning and practising. Better to give each Lancaster aircraft a height to fly, I said, to avoid collisions; a staggered time of take-off and then, as though they were flying at night (at which they were all experienced) send them off not in tight formation but in a loose gaggle, each crew being responsible for finding, identifying and bombing the target, as was the current practice in night flying.

As we broke for lunch, two Australian Wing Commanders came up to me. "You'll either be a Wing Commander or a Sergeant in a week's time", said one. After lunch we re-assembled, and the A.O.C.[3] 5 Group, Air Vice Marshal Sir Ralph Cochrane, joined the conference to hear a report on the morning's session. S.A.S.O. reported that it had all gone well until an outrageous young Flight Lieutenant, the most junior officer in the room, had categorised the whole scheme as impossible. Cochrane stopped him, and requested that the "young officer" should explain his objections in person. This I did. S.A.S.O.'s scheme was rejected, and the Staff were ordered urgently to draw up a plan for daylight bombing based upon my rapidly drawn-up strategy.

The next day Cochrane sent for me. It turned out that he was the younger son of a Scottish radical Earl, and knew a surprising amount about my political activities. As I went out, he said: "Collect another stripe as you go past the stores. You are now a Squadron Leader". Two weeks later he again sent for me to tell me that I was to form a new squadron, later given the number 227, with the rank of Wing Commander.

---

[3] A.O.C – Air Officer Commanding

Thus I had progressed, mainly through incredible good fortune, from being a homeless, jobless, outcast at the age of 16, chucked out of home and obliged to leave school. Seven years later I was a married man and with His Majesty's Commission in the Army. Four years after that, by 1944, I had transferred to the R.A.F., been promoted four times, and was now commanding a heavy bomber squadron with the rank of Wing Commander.

Looked at baldly set out like this, I find the transition very hard to believe. I never sought the significant changes that came my way. I had the self-confidence, and happily developed the skills, to take advantage of the chain of serendipitous circumstances which led to appointments and promotions, and was content – because I had no urge for anything different – with the minimum 'things' which my new status called for.

* * *

Wealthy and good-natured civilians like to lionise men and women who have reached some status, especially in war-time, in the military services. They do this by inviting senior officers to dinner, or to lavish parties, at their homes. One such was Dennis Kendall, M.P. for Grantham, a very successful local businessman. As a Wing Commander and C.O. of a Lancaster squadron based at Balderton, a wartime airfield between Grantham and Newark, I was invited to one of these parties. During the course of the evening, I overheard a somewhat scurrilous conversation between the host and the Liberal M.P. for Eye in Suffolk – later to become a Labour peer and to live to the remarkable age of 102. They were plotting the downfall in the House of the newly formed CommonWealth, and especially of Sir Richard Acland, the founder and President of CommonWealth.[4]

I was scandalised at this unparliamentary political activity, and telephoned the secretary of CommonWealth to inform him of what I had overheard. He was a London solicitor, R.W.G. 'Kim' Mackay. He asked me if, next time I was in London, I would call on him. Eventually I did so. I left with the undertaking that if there was no chance of being

---

[4] This was the name of the political party. J.B. Priestley was very anxious to be in at the beginning a new Party, but others prevailed and the word 'party' was not used. At one time it was called Forward March, after a book title of Acland's, 'The Forward March of the Common People'.

elected, I would be prepared to have my name put forward as a Parliamentary candidate. I had almost completed a tour of operational flying, and thought that it would make a pleasant change from 'flying a desk' or going back to instructing, to being a candidate for Parliament, especially as CommonWealth had a splendid record of *not* being elected. I had no desire to become an M.P.

A few weeks later the Tory M.P. for Chelmsford was flying back to the U.K. to prepare for the General Election, which was due in a few months' time. He made an aerial detour to visit his old regiment in Italy. His aircraft was shot down and he was killed. Thus there came a vacancy for an M.P. in Chelmsford. I was asked if I would like to be considered as a candidate. I concurred, but said that I could not come to a selection meeting in London as I was hotly engaged in running a squadron. They said that a selection committee would come to me, and we fixed the time of a train to Newark which I would meet.

Military duty meant that I had to brief my squadron before lunch, then rush off to the station, talk to the selection committee, then rush back for take-off. It was impossible to put off the visitors, as they had already left, so when I met them I had to tell them that I could only spare fifteen minutes. We went into the station waiting room. They asked a few questions, and then I had to terminate the meeting and return to military duties. To my astonishment, I received notice that I had been selected and was the adopted CommonWealth candidate for the forthcoming Chelmsford by-election.

What nobody had calculated was that there had been no election since 1936. From being a Tory stronghold Chelmsford had developed a considerable increase in manufacturing activity, with companies like Marconi, Hoffman Ballbearings and many other armament-orientated industries with the attendant influx of thousands of industrial workers from all parts of the country. In the event we turned a 16,500 majority in 1936 to a 6,500 majority for CommonWealth. The wartime electoral truce between the three major political parties – no party ran a candidate against the nominee of the party which the late member had represented – meant that neither the Labour nor the Liberal Party had put up a candidate.

So, in April 1945 I duly took my seat as the youngest member of the House of Commons.[5]

---

[5] Ernest was elected at the age of 29 years and 70 days on April 26th 1945.

I am starting to write this autobiography at the age of 87. Unfortunately I have never kept a diary; my R.A.F. logbook is in a museum (alas, I have forgotten which one); papers and photographs relevant to specific items of my life no longer exist, and my memory is not my strongest feature (it would be hard to say what is!) If there were to be any kind (or unkind) readers who have different recollections, I ask them to be generous to the faulty memory of an old man, and to accept that I have sought to be as honest as possible.

Were anyone to be hurt, please accept my apologies. It is, however, *my* life I am endeavouring to write. I freely acknowledge that others may, indeed probably will, have different perspectives. I do not intend or wish to cause hurt.

1

Much has been told in story, poetry and film of the horrors experienced by the men in World War One. It must have been terrible. I can find little about the sufferings of the women who were left, constantly in fear for the safety of their men, struggling to bring up their families on inadequate allowances, considering themselves fortunate if they were able to earn some sort of modest income working in armament factories, taking men's places in engineering works or on the land. Because they were women their rates of pay were low, their working conditions disgraceful, safety standards often minimal with attendant health risks, and yet they were keeping 'the home fires burning' and producing weapons and ammunition for the front. Their many tasks were carried out heroically whilst the men were being sacrificed in an ill-led carnage overseas.

I do not know precisely what my mother, Emily Craggs, did during the war. What I do know is that she was born on 31st October 1884. She was the youngest of a family of seven. Her mother was left a widow, but with a small greengrocery business near the Elephant and Castle. She engaged as manager a man somewhat younger than herself, a merry fellow called Fearnley, who entertained us all at the many parties we seem to have had throughout the year. A favourite wheeze of his at Christmas time was to dress up as a Chinaman with long pig-tails and moustaches. He would then caper and sing, manoeuvring himself until he was under the thickest collection of paper chains. With great dexterity he would swing his head from side to side, then round and round, all the time singing and rotating his body. This would get faster and faster until the pigtails were almost upright from his head and would smash through the paper chains until a large section of them was demolished; an activity more warmly welcomed by the many children at the party than by the adults.

Emily was a shy girl but clearly, at an age when compulsory school attendance stopped at twelve, she had learnt some quite sophisticated mathematics, which she did not reveal to her husband when she got married, and a love of reading which lasted throughout her long life. Like so many young girls of her era she went into domestic service and continued to study cookery, which had been another of her major interests and achievements at school.

While this capable, serious, modest and introverted girl was growing into a reliable and skilful cook, her complementary significant-other was growing into manhood. Complementary because he was her converse in temperament and mannerisms. As a very young child Edmund (Ned) Millington was what used to be called a 'holy terror'. He was strong and fit for his age. Both his parents had died, and he was being brought up by an elder sister. His life was sport orientated and according to family legend, when he wasn't kicking a ball with his mates he was swimming very expertly in the waters of Portsmouth harbour. His pranks made him known to the police who he often escaped by diving fully clad into the harbour.[6] Came the day when his sister was courted and wed by a Welshman who took her off to live in Cardiff. At a guess, by the time of her marriage young Ned was in his teens and his sister and her husband had no desire to take him to South Wales – a decision with which he must heartily have concurred.

He was tall for his age, strong, and showed considerable skills in those team games that called for a very physical approach. As he was now virtually homeless he made the decision which was to determine the next several years of his life. According to family legend, he falsified his age and joined the Army. It was his metier. There was abundant opportunity for a very physical life. The regiment he joined, the Fifth Inniskillen Dragoon Guards, offered him the ordered and disciplined life which, as a young orphan, he had missed out on. He rapidly learned another physical skill, at which he came to excel, riding horses, and together with the arts of war he had opportunity for sport and travel.

His regiment took him to South Africa and then to India. Such leave as he was allowed was spent in Portsmouth, where he played in goal

---

[6] Local newspapers record that in one of his escapades, at the age of about 14, he evaded the police and swam from Portsmouth harbour to the Isle of Wight, a distance of about 6 miles with very fast running tides. Later, he played both Rugby and Association football for the Army and, in 1911, he played in both forms of football for England. He was goalkeeper at soccer and fullback at rugger, both positions which gave great satisfaction to his aggressive physical nature.

for the newly formed Portsmouth Football Club, and in London where he met, amongst others, the Craggs family. On one leave he became engaged to the second from youngest daughter, Amelia, who became my Aunt Amy. The Regiment was posted to India. Whilst he was there, he became the centre of a soothsaying prophecy that Emily, the youngest and the prettiest of the Craggs girls, who was more interested in advancing her safe and satisfying career as a cook, would eventually be engaged to and marry a man who was at that time overseas, but already engaged to marry another young woman. He returned with his Regiment, broke off his engagement with Amy, and paid strong court to Emily. It is small wonder that a family with such splendid Victorian names as Louisa, Eleanor, Amelia, Emily, Charles and James were horrified at his perfidy, and that he was never forgiven, even after his marriage to Emily who, possibly under the influence of the soothsayer's prophecy, eventually gave in. They were duly wed. Babies came along at a steady rate: Charles in 1912, Dorothy in 1914, I myself in 1916, Evelyn in 1920 and James in 1928.

One of the effects of war, both World War One and World War Two, was that men home on leave found their young wives very preoccupied with the heavy task of raising a young family, In our case it took the form of father having a very close and tender relationship with his daughters and a fierce but controlled hostility, probably jealousy-inspired, with his sons. When my elder brother, who was born with a malformed left hand and both feet also somewhat crippled, was about 16 he was turned out of the house. I think my mother intervened as strongly as her nature permitted on behalf of her disabled first-born. Four years later, as I will record, I was ordered out. My brother only stayed away for about two weeks, then was taken back and was in close contact with both parents, and under father's thumb, until their demise. On the other hand, I did not crawl back. There were other more blatant reasons for our mutual hostility which I will deal with later. I neither saw my father nor exchanged a word with him for the next nine or ten years. Only when I achieved a commission in the Royal Artillery did I discover that he had become prone, in conversation with his mates, to attribute outrageous opinions – his own, of course – to "my boy, the Army officer".

In the autumn of 1919 my mother became pregnant with my next sibling. Apparently Mother was having a difficult time, so sent me to school with my elder brother with a request that I be permitted to stay for a week or so. One great gift I had obtained from my literate mother was that I had begun to read and write, although I was not four years old until the following February.

The school, Loxford Infants' School in Ilford, Essex, had as headmistress a Miss Thompson. I can remember only two things about her. First, by an extraordinary feat of memory, I can recollect her address – Galara, Great Gearies, Barkingside. I think the memory owes much to my fascination with words. The other, less happy memory is that one day I was the end child in the line of my class in the playground, waiting to be led into school. In a fit of exuberance I did a twirl. Next to me was Miss Thompson who gave me a resounding smack on the leg. On my first day she asked me how old I was. I thought she meant how old I would be on my birthday in February. She misinterpreted my reply, "Four", as meaning that I was now four years old and would be five in a few weeks' time and, as I could already read and write a little and would be no drag on the Infants' teacher, I was allowed to stay on. I was put on the register as a five year old on my fourth birthday.

Emily, Ernest's mother

By coincidence there was a small boy about to start school the following term named Bob Lillington. Although he later turned out to be good at games, when he started he had a leg in irons and was often away for treatment. Come the next term, the teacher called the register. She reached Lillington. He wasn't there. I heard a name which I thought was mine and answered "Present, Miss", and so on the first day of the term before my fourth birthday I was officially present as a five-year old! This extra year of grace lasted me throughout my school career. I 'went up' to the 'Big School' at 10 years old, sat the county scholarship at the same age, and was qualified for secondary education at 10 instead of 11. This gap was acknowledged by the Essex County Council Education Committee and I was permitted to take the scholarship exam, which determined the status of the school, Grammar or Elementary, to which I would go in September. To my total astonishment, which would have been just as great if I had been eleven, I was listed as third in the exam in the whole of the county of Essex. Dumb lot, Essex kids!

At this juncture I must go back to my father. When we were very small, the resentment he felt against his sons was held in reasonable restraint. He was having a 'good war'. By that, one means he was surviving and being promoted. He started the war as a Sergeant, a high rank for a thirty year old. He rose to Warrant Officer Class One (Regimental Sergeant Major) and was awarded the Military Medal and the Distinguished Conduct Medal for his service during the Great War.

One event in his life which was to have a profound effect later was the decision to terminate the engagement of regular soldiers in 1914, to re-employ them in the same rank with immediate effect. Their service prior to this bizarre arrangement was not to count for pension qualification. Thus Sergeant Millington lost 14 years which might well have contributed to making him eligible for a reasonable pension for the rest of his life. This was not to be. At the time, being a High Tory, he thought that this was a superb piece of Government skill, a view which changed considerably in the post war depression years.

He was demobilised in 1918 with no experience but his military and sporting record. So he decided that, with his cavalry experience, he would apply for the mounted division of the Metropolitan Police. Apparently he sailed through the formal interviews, and was faced only with a medical. Again according to legend, the appropriate medical waiting room was full of confident ex soldiers, all eager to get through to the last stage and playful, as only self-confident healthy men all together in the nude can be. Just as his name was called for the eyesight test a skylarking fellow candidate flicked him about the head with a damp towel. The end of it went into his eye, causing much watering and leaving the eye bloodshot. He failed the medical on the eyesight test. So he was left with no employable civilian skills in a period when the labour market was crowded with demobilised soldiers, all willing to do anything to earn a living.

One of the officers of the regiment was a relative of the proprietor of the Evening Standard. He was introduced, interviewed and offered regular employment by that newspaper. The two essential requirements for mass printing, apart from the paper itself, were ink, which had to be kept at a regular malleability and fluency, and the metal from which the letters were formed to make up the printed word. My father was employed in the stores which controlled supplies of ink and the printing metal.

One day a workman was crossing a plank walkway which went across a vast vat of boiling metal. The plank slipped, and the man seized the only thing to hand, which was the strong, copper conductor bar which carried the current to the printing presses. The man fainted. His hand convulsed onto the live bar. He was locked in suspension over a lethal vat of boiling metal. Somebody ran to switch off the current. My father barged him out of the way and explained that if the current were switched off, he would uncurl his fingers and fall into the vat. A net was hastily slung underneath him, and he was lowered to safety and rushed to St Bartholomew's Hospital, just round the corner, and survived. Old 'Inky' was the hero of the hour, a status which gave rise to promotion by the employers, and election as Father of the Chapel – chairman of the executive committee of the local branch of his union, NATSOPA.[7]

At the General Strike of 1926 it was clear that if everybody came out on strike, the vats of metal would grow cold and solidify. As it would take at least eight days for them to come back to pouring temperature, the strikers would have to be locked out for a week after the termination of the strike. Somebody who knew precisely what to do had to break the strike and come to work. Management and work-force agreed that the man who knew what had to be done and could be trusted to do it not just in the interest of the employers, but for everyone's sake, was the Chairman of the Union branch, the F.O.C. So my father was one of the few in that devastating piece of nationally coordinated industrial action who worked by the agreement of all sides. (I have never been able to understand why stopping work is not called industrial *in*action).

At precisely that time I had passed the county scholarship sufficiently high in the list to be offered interviews by a number of schools. By this time my father was determined to do nothing to further

---

[7] The National Society of Operative Printers and Assistants

my education. My mother discovered that I could get to Chigwell by a 'pirate' company – that is, one running unscheduled buses, manned by non-union crews – which went from Ilford Broadway to Chigwell Row. I could easily walk to Ilford Broadway, and the school was about two miles from the nearest point reached by the bus. My mother confirmed our appointment with the Headmaster, by letter I suspect, and off I went, aged ten, unaccompanied by an adult as my mother had other children at home to look after, to find a school which none of us had ever seen, and to present myself for what one might now call a 'viva'. I set off clutching the shilling piece taken from the housekeeping purse, to an unknown destination. I had been told to ask to be put off at a pub called the Bald Hind. "Ah", said the conductor, "You mean the Bare Arse".

I found the road in which Chigwell School had stood for almost three hundred years. There were some boys going in the right direction, kicking a football. They invited me to join in. What nobody had told me was that the village elementary school was in the same road as the Grammar School. I joined in, and dusty and flushed presented myself, armed with the letter confirming my appointment, to the headmaster of the wrong school. He must have been a nice man. He lent me a shoe brush and brushed my jacket, let me rinse my hands and face and showed me where to go for my interview.

Years later when I became M.P. for Chelmsford I discovered that one of my constituents was the former headmaster of Chigwell. He told me that when I appeared before him unaccompanied by an adult and told him about the strike, and the boys in the road and the football, and the kind headmaster of the other school, he determined to offer me a free place. In the event I was able to give a reasonable answer to his one vaguely academic request, "With your finger in the air trace the outline of England, naming the counties as you pass them". I don't know if I did well or not, but I was accepted, and started at Chigwell the following September.

2

Chigwell School was founded by a former Archbishop of York when he was Vicar of Chigwell, a village on the Essex outskirts of London. It had one famous building, the King's Head Inn, locally reputed to have been a favourite haunt of Charles Dickens – a claim disputed by another King's Head Inn at Chigwell Row, about two miles away. The school had built up a growing academic and sporting record. The staff, as I remember them, were almost all bachelors, dedicated to the task of educating boys, mainly in the classics, and preparing them for university entrance.

In my day, two magnificent seniors had gone to Oxford. Their names were Smythe and Papineau and before I left we celebrated them each obtaining a double first class honours degree. We also had a mathematics genius, Eric Primrose, who was determined to go to Cambridge and become Senior Wrangler in Mathematics. This he achieved in circumstances which had a considerable long-term effect on the school. This began with his mother, a fragile young widow who was determined that nothing would stand in the way of her only son achieving his ambition. Primrose had come to the school about three years after me, also on a county scholarship. The school being by tradition and staffing a specialist classics school, he rose rapidly in Latin, Greek and English, but also with startling results in Maths. So that at the age of sixteen he had the necessary Ordinary and Higher Schools Certificates to go on to university. At this stage his mother turned up by appointment to discuss his future. "He will go on scholarship to Cambridge and read Maths. He will become Senior Wrangler", she said. The Maths department was consulted and although it was clear that they were perfectly capable of continuing to succeed in training the boys to obtain their Higher Schools Certificates they had neither the necessary personal background nor the experience to teach Primrose to the level required.

Not at all put out, the mother reported that she had been in communication with another school, Wolverhampton Grammar School, who said they would be delighted to take her son on, transferring his scholarship. Not unnaturally, the staff at Chigwell were loathe to let a genius go, but could not guarantee the quality of the teaching he required. The dilemma was widely discussed in the staff room when John Doouss, who was the rather retiring head of the English department, shyly announced that his hobby was working out problems in higher mathematics. Investigation revealed that he had covered, for personal pleasure, most of the areas which Thurston, head of Maths, felt that nobody in his department could teach.

John Doouss, of Norwegian origin, was a very remarkable man. He had left school at twelve and worked on the land, first as a ploughboy, then as a general farm hand. At the age of twenty one he unexpectedly inherited a fairly large amount of money. This, he decided, would be put entirely into furthering his own education. Very quickly, some say within three years, he was able to take up a place on an English degree course at Oxford. By the age of thirty he had graduated. In those days such courses as the Post Graduate Certificate in Education did not exist. A graduate with a good degree – and some with less good degrees – could start work, without further training, as a teacher. Doouss went to Chigwell, where he prospered. He was a natural though somewhat formal teacher, and he became head of the English department. Then came the Primrose crisis. Mr Doouss agreed to take the young genius on. Still continuing as Head of English he devoted the rest of his time to teaching and coaching Primrose who stayed on at Chigwell, obtained the appropriate entry qualifications to read Maths at Cambridge and became, in due course, Senior Wrangler. John Doouss for a time became Head of Maths as well as Head of English, a unique situation for any school of academic repute.

It would be remiss of me to leave the impression that the only member of the teaching staff whom I remember with any clarity is John Doouss. He was a most remarkable man and worthy of recollection. There were, of course, others who stay in my memory.

First and foremost the headmaster, E.H. Stewart Walde. He was an impressive figure of a man, about six foot tall, good shoulders and upright carriage. There was an Imposition School every Wednesday afternoon. Boys caught out in wickedness spent the afternoon in a punishment room, under supervision, carrying out such tasks as were imposed by the teachers responsible for their committal. Into this would come the Headmaster, clutching under his arm a small cluster of canes and a punishment book. I had three occasions to be one of those awaiting the dire punishment. I can only remember the reason for one visit. We had done our end of term examinations. I had done well. Passing the Geography teacher's desk I saw that the top paper in a pile of marked completed examination papers was in my handwriting. So I leant over to see if I could catch a glimpse of a mark. I did. 82%. I was top in Geography; the papers were in order of merit.

Mr Grant came in and saw me looking at his desk. I hadn't touched anything. I wouldn't have dared. So I was sent for detention the following Wednesday afternoon. In came the Headmaster. My name was called. I was ordered out to the front and told to bend over a desk. I received four strokes of the cane on my bottom – for looking at a teacher's desk. It is rumoured that the Headmaster kept his hand in by chopping down trees in a paddock at the far end of the school grounds. I had good reason to believe that the rumour was true.

I have mentioned Mr Grant: Mr D.P. Grant, known of course as 'Dippy'. He was a smallish man, very smartly dressed and with a neatly trimmed Ronald Coleman moustache. It is said that he was immensely ambitious with an ambition that went miles beyond being a one-man department of Geography in a small minor public school. To this end he had studied for the church and, while I was still at Chigwell, he was ordained a minister of the Church of England. He then got married and added to his academic qualifications for promotion to a headship in a C. of E. secondary school the advantages of being a married priest. I have no idea what became of him but I wished him well in spite of the beating I got for looking at his desk.

Of greater significance in my life at school was Arnold Fellows. When I went to Chigwell he must still have been only thirty years of age plus or minus a year or so. He was tall with a very large head covered in white hair. He could have been prematurely aged but, in fact, was one of the most energetic and active men I ever met. He taught history to all classes but made it interesting at every level. I can see him now sweeping into a classroom on November 5th, removing a boy in the front row so that he could sit on the desk with his feet on the seat, and opening a discussion on 'What would have been the consequence if Guy Fawkes had been successful?' In such a way he captured our close attention (or mine, anyway), and I learnt more than I think I could possibly have got from a textbook about the conflict in England in the sixteenth and early seventeenth centuries between Catholics and Protestants. It still informs, for example, my attitude towards the conflict in Northern Ireland. It is a struggle for power cloaked under the disguise of religious fervour.

But Mr Fellows was not only a great teacher. He took all ages in the school for football. He was well qualified. He played for a somewhat elitist club known as the Corinthians. To qualify for membership one had to have been a public schoolboy and then a University graduate. We all felt a reflected glow of pride when the Corinthians reached the semi-final of the F.A. Amateur Cup and *our* teacher played for them.

Another character amongst the staff was Father Charles Kay. He was the school chaplain and taught Latin, especially to the lower forms. He drove around the school and district in a Trojan car, a small vehicle with a very noisy two-stroke engine. Nowadays comedians have a constantly repeated catchphrase by which they are known. If Father Kay had been with us today he would have been known for his. Every evening that he set his quota of Prep (homework for day boys) he would finish off by saying, "Don't smuggle in fairy stories or other teachers' prep. I want from each of you *forty minutes' solid grind.*" He didn't get it, but was known throughout the school as 'Solid Grind'. He was very popular because he ran the school tuck-shop. Every day at lunch and break-times he was there dispensing chocolate bars and soft drinks. I look back on this as just another voluntary unpaid extra duty carried out day after day for years by some already overworked teachers.

The saddest memory I have is of Mr H.D. ('D'Arcy') Wells, the French teacher. In a school which specialised in the study of classical Latin and Greek, French was not regarded as a very serious academic option. I read it by choice because of my love of words. D'Arcy Wells not only encouraged this love but was always delighted from time to time to talk about such topics as the philosophy of the French Revolution and how it all went wrong. Under his influence I was glad to have taken Higher School certificate in French. He had soldiered through the First World War. When the Second World War broke out he could not face up to the thought that all those boys with whom he had worked might experience what he had gone through or worse. So he committed suicide. Excruciatingly sad.

The well-equipped laboratories were in a field on the opposite side of the road from the main school. The Head of Science had also been through the First World War and still retained a commissioned rank in the Territorial Army. When I first went to Chigwell he was Captain Dyball. Before I left he had been promoted to Major. As an Army man I suspect he felt that he had a role to play as a disciplinarian. His lessons were severely structured but, to the non-scientific schoolboys, very interesting. For example in 1930 aircraft were comparatively rare. If one flew over his lab he would allow the class to go outside to look at it. On our return we would have an interesting and informed introduction to aerodynamics, a subject *not* on the curriculum.

These were some of the men who made a sufficient impression on me that I can still recall something significant about them. There were others too. G.B. Stott (who could not have been more than five or six years older than me) came straight from Cambridge and joined as the most junior member of staff, teaching classical Greek. I met him during the War. He was a non-flying R.A.F. officer with the rank of Squadron Leader. I was a Wing Commander. I called him 'Sir' because he had been my teacher for a short time at school. He called me 'Sir' by virtue of my senior rank. Neither of us thought it at all funny. I heard from him again many years later. He had seen my name in 'Who's Who' and wrote apologising for having mentioned me in a book without obtaining my permission. As if I cared. In the tradition of bachelor public school masters he had just got married, for the first time, at the age of ninety.

When I was in the Upper Fifth the Greek set consisted of only six boys. We were taught in the oldest building in the school, a tiny room smaller than the average suburban sitting room, which featured a pot-bellied coal burning stove in one corner of the room. By rearranging our desks we could hem the teacher in the corner by the stove. A dexterous-footed boy in the nearest desk could pump the fire up surreptitiously with his foot until the top of the stove shone an incandescent red. A boy called Marsh become adept at this art. We were able to get rid of two young teachers straight from University in one autumn term. The first was a rather wet young man who had no control at all. We took it in turns to ask whether we could go the school library to borrow an enormous volume of the Liddell and Scott Greek/English dictionary. Permission would be granted and the pupil stagger back with the large book. He would have looked up a word which we were not supposed to know and then ask the teacher a personal question such as, "Sir. Are you a *paidesteres*?", literally 'lover of boys'. The teacher, a Mr Thomas, if I remember rightly, dismissed the class. I was the last to go out and as I went through the door he said to me quite fiercely, "Paidesteres means bugger – tell your little friends". He did not last after half term.

He was followed by an equally inexperienced young man. By this time it was well into autumn. The pot-bellied stove was lit. Desks were moved closer. Marsh got to work with the pump. The teacher was forced closer to the stove. The second time it smoked his gown burst into flames. The teacher ran out of the room tearing off his gown. We never saw him again.

So there they were, some marvellous teachers to whom one is eternally grateful, some pitiful failures who, one hopes, decided that teaching was not their profession.

* * *

It was to this small but highly successful minor public school that I reported in September 1926, at the age of ten. The school was organised in three phases – Lower, Middle and Upper. Lower School, Forms 1 and 2, was for younger boys, building up the standards at the age of ten to eleven, before entering the Middle School. Here the structure was more complicated. Everybody started at eleven in Form 3. One must remember that there was no policy of selection in those days. The qualifications for admission were two-fold, either you had a father who could afford to pay the fees or you had won a scholarship. Form 3 therefore manifested a fine example of mixed ability teaching.

The staff worked hard to sort out the faster and lower streams, and they duly formed the next two classes in Middle School, Forms 4a and 4b. Form 4b was for pupils who needed an extra year before being considered for a more advanced syllabus. Next came a Form called the Remove. If a pupil was still not ready for the more taxing work he could mark time in the Remove for yet another year being going on to the Upper School. Upper School consisted of Forms 5a and 5b and Sixth Form. Once again a bright boy could go direct from 4a to 5a. 5b existed to enable slower learners an extra year to prepare for Sixth Form and public examinations. This structure enabled the quick learner to leap up the scholastic ladder leaving out the extra years put in to help the slow learner. I must have been a 'quickie'. I spent a year, at the age of ten, in Form 3 and then went bounding up through 4a and 5a, reaching the Sixth form at the age of fourteen.

Fortunately I was big for my age, and tough. A lot of the local boys were the sons of farmers and minor landowners. They were well-off and often rather stupid. So I found myself with one or two other bright lads in classes where the average age was two to three years older than we were. My recollections are of delight at the academic side of my life but something close to despair from time to time at the social life. Surrounded by bigger, richer and older boys who hated 'swots' I was happy to be able to look after myself. When I was in 4a, perhaps twelve years old, there was one really nasty son of a local farmer, aged fourteen or fifteen, named Fuller. In a fit of candour I must have responded honestly to the question of what my father's occupation was. Somehow Fuller discovered that my father worked for the Evening Standard and was responsible for ink stores there. This amused Master Fuller, who went around telling everybody that my father's job was filling the inkwells of a newspaper. Had I been a little more mature, perhaps I could have laughed it off, but this snobbish little lout would not leave it alone and went on day after day, inventing scurrilous and degrading stories about my father – whom, incidentally, I really disliked and who did nothing to support and sustain me. One day Fuller went too far. So I hit him. He, of course, ran to the headmaster, who sent for me. I went in and was asked for an explanation. I seem to remember that I was quite tense. "He was very rude about my father, and would not shut up. So I hit him." The headmaster looked at me severely and said, "I have only one complaint about your conduct. You didn't hit him hard enough".

It was at Chigwell that learnt a great deal about self-awareness and self-control, as well as covering a syllabus designed to prepare the student for University entrance. I must have been the poorest boy in the school because I had no support at all from my father. I alone had no personal games clothes. I managed by being fitted out from the Lost Property bin. When, in my final year, I was promoted to Vice Prefect, I alone could not wear the appropriate headgear, a specially tailored straw hat with the ribbon varied to denote House or School team colours. But it is not painful to remember those few years, as they were years of success and achievement. I played football for the school and football and cricket for my House. Most of all, though, I enjoyed the school work. It was not only the languages which fascinated but the content of work by great scholars of the past. I can still quote from Homer's Odyssey, Virgil's Aeneid and Plato's Republic. Less impact was made on me by the French, but I recollect some Voltaire and Racine, lines which come back from time to time into my head. A combination of Plato and Voltaire must have contributed largely to the development of the radical philosophies which have bound me ever since.

3

It is a fairly frequent phenomenon that when one wants to recollect a journey, especially if the wish is to describe it in writing, one recalls the circumstances of the start of the journey and a detailed description of its end. Large parts of the space between become vague and misty round the edges. So it is with this stage in my journey in life. I can and will describe how it was that at sixteen I set off homeless and with no money and no job. It will not be difficult for me to describe where I had arrived when war broke out in 1939, by which time I had become a young Army officer, with a commission as 2nd Lieutenant in the Royal Artillery, and married with a wife and child. Clearly significant events took place in between. The causes of these events preceded them.

First I must describe the point at which I had arrived in August 1932. My father had always been hostile to his two elder sons, one born just before the First World War and the other, me, in early 1916. Father must have done well in the Army, especially during the War. As he rose in the ranks, his authority over his subordinates grew more absolute. As a Warrant Officer, 1st class (R.S.M)[8], he had reached the highest possible rank below that of a commissioned officer. All solders, from sergeants down to privates, called him "Sir". He had reached a peak of professional promotion. In those days promotion from non-commissioned or warrant to commissioned rank, even for R.S.M.s, was very uncommon. In another context one might go on at length about the snobbishness which reached its apex in the hierarchical structure of the armed forces. Here a callow and often unintelligent scion of an old military family, both his grandfather and his great grandfather were generals, gave orders to soldiers whose distinguished service had begun before the newly commissioned officer was born.

The sergeants and sergeants major, trained now to receive instant

---

[8] Regimental Sergeant Major

respect and obedience, came home to find alien young males who gave manifestation of total devotion to their mothers. This seemed to have been reciprocated, often at the expense of the tenderness expected by the soldier, especially when he was on an infrequent leave from a tense and dangerous situation. One sympathises with the feeling of the soldier, but understands that a young mother, bringing up a small family and often, *because* of her feelings for the father, showing what must have appeared to be greater intimacy with boy babies, who continued to sleep with their mothers, sometimes until four or even five years old, often at the expense of the father. Then as the babies grew into boyhood their fathers, who commanded respect and instant obedience from any number of grown men, received the inevitable, traditional resistance of the young to their progenitors. This normal and virtually universal situation must have come more harshly to those who in their domestic situation sought to exercise the authority which obtained in working life.

I think it may be worthwhile to digress for a moment to examine the concepts to which I refer. It is easy to use the words 'authority' and 'power' as though they were interchangeable. 'Authority' derives from the Latin 'auctoritas' and implies that which is a consequence of role. There is an element almost of the magical associated with the word. Thus a weak man becomes stronger if he wears the uniform of a policeman. Even the mere wearing of a recognised uniform will confer authority. People in a crowd round the victim of a street accident will automatically make way for a man in uniform, even if he is a postman or a train driver. 'Power' derives also from the Latin; 'potens' means 'being able to…'

The most common cause of tension in any hierarchical set-up is one in which the person expected to wield the greatest influence, because of the 'authority' conferred by rank, has under his jurisdiction people whose potential (another splendid power word) is greater than that of their boss or bosses by virtue of their innate 'power' i.e. what they feel and know they can do. So it was with men back from the wars. Skill and application to the military arts might have brought about promotion. Promotion – to corporal, then sergeant and then perhaps to sergeant major – gave responsibility over a growing number of men.

In the military forces there is a centuries-old tradition reinforcing authority over subordinates. N.C.O.s[9] on leave, or in the insecure days of

---

[9] Non Commissioned Officers

trying to settle into domestic life and civilian employment, found that they could not get from their children the instant respect and obedience that had been their wont in the services. One therefore has, almost universally, a separation between child, especially son, and father. One is particularly moved by the problem experienced by those who returned at the end of the war having been prisoners of war for months or even years. There are well authenticated stories of such soldiers referring to themselves as "your Daddy" only to be told cruelly, "You are not my Daddy. There is my Daddy", pointing to a much treasured by now out of date photograph on the wall. This kind of uncaring attitude, amounting almost to rejection, might with patience have been diminished, but coupled with the different expectations of child and father towards the mother often settled into a steady undercurrent of a ridiculous but very real kind of suppressed sexual jealousy.

We all grow older, children at a faster rate than adults. As the infant becomes a toddler, and the toddler a young schoolchild, the desire of the child to share marvellous newly acquired knowledge and skills may be resented if the opportunity to develop such skills had eluded the father. The gap may grow as the sophistication of what is being learned increases.

* * *

In my case my father had spent almost five years in France during the war. He had been surrounded daily by signs and posters in French, but his daily language of communication of course was English. Commonplace French expressions were absorbed into daily use but often mispronounced as misheard, or converted to a more English sounding version. For example, 'Ca ne fait rien' became 'san fairy ann', and 'il n'y a plus' became 'na poo'.

When I began to learn French I would come home eager to communicate my wonderful new skills but, alas, equally eager to correct the errors in precision or pronunciation when my father, at first eagerly, tried to air what he had learned. After all, he had learned his French during a long residence in France. He would get angry at being corrected by one who should, in the proper order of things, be politely and respectfully accepting and obeying. Even after sixty-odd years, I can well remember making a decision not to argue or press a point, and then being punished for that most nebulous but lethal of service crimes – 'dumb insolence'.

I realise now that as I progressed through secondary education I would come home filled with new knowledge, language, science, history and even the geography of those parts of France in which he had lived, but could not set into a national, regional or continental context. Any display of knowledge inevitably led to furious quarrels which I now believe to have been due to frustration and educational jealousy. One must not forget that he had been a most successful soldier and leader of men. Now he was a poorly paid unskilled labourer and all his ideas and beliefs were being regularly challenged by a half-grown lad (although he was to make some progress in responsibility and income in the near future).

In a way it was fortunate that my siblings had been born in the order boy-girl-boy-girl-boy. The eldest was my lovely partly disabled big brother.[10] During World War One cards were available at the front pre-printed 'To My Dear Wife', 'To Mother' and, in the event of the eldest – or only – child being a boy, 'To My Chum'. My brother had a collection of these cards, which he treasured all his life. His nickname was 'Chum', although his wife when he got married insisted on calling him Charles. During the formative days of World War One and in the immediate post-war years my relationship with my father was softened a little by the fact that his first born was specially cosseted, and quite rightly so, by my mother. In addition, when I came along I grew up between two bouncing and charming sisters, whom my father preferred to me. [11]

---

[10] Edmund Charles – Chum – was born with a defective left hand and problems with both feet. The fingers of his left hand were less than half the length and thickness of 'normal' fingers and they were joined together, making a small hand with fingers that could not articulate singly. All his life, though not outwardly self-conscious, he tended to wear a glove on his left hand. Both his feet suffered from the same defect as his hand. The feet were shrunken, the toes very short and webbed. He must never have worn shoes bigger than size 5 or 6 and never, to my knowledge, was able to run or play any games or sports. I never once heard him complain. He quickly learnt to drive cars, especially big ones. He became mace bearer and Rolls Royce chauffeur for the Mayor of Ilford and finished his local government career as Superintendent of Public Buildings for the Borough of Ilford, with responsibility for maintenance, staffing and letting of the Town Hall, the Swimming Baths and sundry other smaller public buildings.

[11] *Ernest added this amendment some weeks later:*
I have just come off the phone from Eve who tells me that I have got it all

I always knew when something was amiss, however. Under the pretext of giving a valuable lesson in self-defence, he would get out two pairs of boxing gloves. At first he would conduct his side of the transaction sitting on a dining room chair. As I got older he got to his feet and towered over me. I suppose at this time he must have weighed about 16 stone, and he was fairly fit. Consequently the suggestion, "Let's put the gloves on after tea", was greeted not as an unmixed sign of paternal friendship but as a warning that I had done something of which he disapproved, and that I would pay for it before the evening was out.

We struggled on with growing distance between us as I began to develop a very theoretical and altruistic political sense. For example, it worried me enormously – and I can remember at the time being very impressed – that Plato's first class citizen, the Philosopher King, having been selected at an early age for his role, was trained to take his place as a decision-maker and administrator. For this task he would not receive any rewards beyond the living wage for all educated adults. This contrasted sharply with the little I knew about the salaries awarded to themselves by leading politicians, by leaders of industry and even, dare one whisper it, by leaders of the Church.

I also began at almost 14 years old to look deeply into religious thought and practice. There did not seem to be acres of difference between the great world religions in respect of the basic principles of desirable conduct between people. Although the little I was beginning to find out about Buddhism revealed much that I admired and accepted about human relationships I could not find enough teaching to make it an acceptable whole belief system. It attracted me warmly to know that Buddhist monks throughout the world were teaching that it is a duty to resolve international and personal conflict by negotiation and compromise without rushing to have resort to armies and violence. I was not sure about metempsychosis, the belief that each living creature had a

---

wrong. He was obsessed with his elder daughter, Emily Dorothy, whom he called Bingo after the role played in a film by his favourite film star, Joan Crawford. He thought his daughter was like the film star. As far as Eve was concerned she must have answered him back, or refused close contact. He wanted to chuck Eve out when she was sixteen. To which my mother made the memorable and heroic rejoinder, "If she goes, I go". He never addressed another word to Eve until after she was married at 21. He did not attend her wedding.

soul and that when a corporal body died its soul migrated into a newly born body; a belief which solved the vexed problem of the resurrection on Judgement Day of all bodies of believers. Stanley Spencer's famous painting of resurrection, multiplied by the thousands of burial grounds throughout the world, made for an overcrowding which was, and still is, entirely beyond my comprehension.

I attended meetings of both Roman Catholic and Protestant evangelists. Nobody could explain why two great churches, both claiming to be dedicated to the worship of the Prince of Peace, could spend so much blood and money fighting one another for domination. Gradually it dawned on me that the great churches were in fact political organisations. Their principles were preached by leaders who seemed determined to betray the very principles they advocated. 'Religio' means to tie together. Belief systems were advanced and propagated in order to build together, by some mystic belief system, people who were persuaded that they held in common a shared political and economic interest. The history of religion, with magnificent exceptions, was the history of groups who sought a mystical justification for the pursuance of economic aims. Surely political aims could best be achieved by persuading the majority of people to accept agreed beliefs and aspirations and hope to achieve them through political means?

So, at the age of fourteen, I joined the Labour Party League of Youth. Largely because I was enthusiastic and physically strong I was soon given the task of collecting our collapsible speaker's platform and erecting it at agreed open air speaking plots in anticipation of the arrival of the branch chairman, who would act as chairman for a visiting speaker, and for the speaker when he came. One Saturday evening – most of our meetings were open air – I had erected the platform. The crowd began to gather. It consisted of supporters, virulent opponents and a varying number of Saturday evening strollers for whom it was a regular weekly entertainment. At the due time the platform was ready. The speaker but arrived – but there was no chairman.

We waited, but the chairman, one Eric Digby Hunt, who went on to become the secretary of the British History Association, just did not appear. The speaker, Pete Douglas, who was an early propagandist about the danger of Fascism in Italy, Germany and ultimately Great Britain was, in his own view, too important to open a meeting and collect his own crowd. "Up you go", he said to me, for I was obviously keeper of the platform. "Comrades and fellow workers!" I was practically forced on to the rostrum. To my horror, I had barely started when I saw Master

Douglas disappearing into a pub. So my career as a public speaker began when I was about fourteen and a half years old. My first essay was to last about fifteen minutes, until Pete had finished his pint.

Nowadays we don't have regular public meetings in which people come in a more or less orderly fashion to hear events of the day discussed by enthusiasts. Not in those days the vast banner-bestrewn demonstrations which seem to convince nobody and to provide a battleground for people who would rather fight than discuss. I cannot remember much about my initiation. People must have been kind and tolerant. Pete Douglas appeared and the meeting went on its way. I had discovered a new skill. Young as I was I could make people listen to me. For the next four or five years public speaking became my main weekend activity. I acquired quite a reputation as a youth orator and was invited to speak on various open air platforms in and around London.

In particular I recall many meetings I shared with Ted Willis, later Lord Willis and a pillar of the Establishment. Like me, Ted had felt the necessity of enlisting in the Army to fight Fascism, especially in Europe. He was an excellent soldier, amongst other things the champion marksman of his regiment. One day, walking along High Holborn in the uniform I had recently acquired as a 2nd Lieutenant, I saw coming towards me, in civilian clothes, none other than my old friend. He told me a strange tale of woe. He was doing very well as a soldier, and had reached the rank, I seem to remember, of Quartermaster Sergeant. One day he had been sent for urgently by his colonel. Expecting commendation for some activity which had gone surprisingly well, he had reported to him. To his astonishment he was told the order had come down from the War Office that Sergeant Willis was to be discharged with immediate effect from the Army, and was to leave as a civilian before nightfall the same day. Unofficially it was explained that Ted had shown an interest in a body known as the Peoples' Convention, which had been set up to challenge the accepted motives for participation in the war and to discuss alternative ultimate aims. No doubt if the leaders of the Peoples' Convention had been named Beveridge they might have been permitted to do their research and present their report. The Convention took in a wide range of individuals and groups who were actively challenging whether the object of the war was to return as nearly as possible to the status quo ante. Included in their ranks were pacifists, Communists, wild-eyed and wild-haired idealists, and some Trade Union leaders; indeed, those whom one would expect to be challenging the intentions of the current ruling elite. No place for an aspiring young N.C.O. who had, previous to joining up, been an A.E.U.[12] shop steward and a promising Young Socialist.

Ernest aged 16

Ted was offered the management of the Unity Theatre, a run down little theatre in Mornington Crescent that was surviving on a regime of leftish playlets. Under his leadership Unity pioneered many devices which have subsequently become commonplace in the theatre. For example he is believed to have been the first to have had actors enter the theatre through the auditorium, treating the audience as though they were part of the dramatis personae. In one play I remember the audience

---

[12] A.E.U. – Amalgamated Engineering Union

found themselves all to be striking dock-workers and to be reacting vociferously to the speeches of the strikers' leaders. It is theatre history that Ted Willis took every aspect of the theatre in his stride and eventually made his name as a playwright working for the B.B.C.

To go back to our pre-war meetings. Ted ran meetings which I addressed every Friday night at South Tottenham, on the corner of Seven Sisters Road. He would come to me as my guest speaker in Ilford on the following evening.

Our reward was to be treated by the other to fish and chips which, I seem to remember, came to sixpence a portion. This not only provided us with our evening meal but greased tender and over-strained throats. On one Saturday the inevitable happened. Strolling amongst the evening crowds, accompanied by one of my sisters, an interested father paused to listen to the oratory of his second son. When I returned home I was told to leave the next morning and never to return.

Our hostility to one another had been reinforced by my father's very different attitude to politics. Like many a good soldier he had lived through quite a few years in which the sharp distinction between social classes was as clear as the distance between military ranks. It would be no exaggeration to claim that the rightness of class distinction was held and propagated more by the successful N.C.O. than it was by the private soldier, the lumpen proletariat of the Army.

At first father registered his disapproval of the egalitarian philosophy he had heard me advocating by tightening the rules which governed his household. He made it more difficult for me to do my school homework by forcing me, especially in winter, to do it in a poorly gas-lit and unheated room. When I went out in the evenings I was subject to a ten o'clock curfew. This I overcame by standing outside the house and waiting for a local church clock to strike ten. I would wait for the quarters to be struck, then knock on the front door knocker, synchronising my knock with the first of the hours. Not unnaturally I failed to synchronise precisely every time, and each failure added an item to my slate of misdemeanours.

The local church, whose striking of the hours played such an important part in the contest which was being waged with my father, was the Ilford High Road Baptist Church. I had for some time discontinued church attendance but the minister was responsible for a number of activities in which I was involved. His name was the Reverend Charles Vine. He was, I learned later, very well known in academic circles for his self-directed research into Old English. He was not a graduate, but by application had achieved many insights into Old Norse and other sources of Old and Middle English which had gone into books acknowledged in academic circles. Within his church he had initiated and led the formation of a number of community bodies. One was known as the Ilford Men's Meeting. Not only was it an ecumenical meeting for discussion and debate on religious and secular matters but it also had the only Horticultural Society in this fairly populous suburb. Every year the main horticultural events of the year were the Spring and Autumn I.M.M. produce shows.

My father had taken on two plots of allotment in a very favourable position about a mile and a half from our house. They were side by side, the first two plots on the left as one entered the area devoted to the growth of vegetables and soft fruits. Immediately ahead was a straight path which led to a stream from which one could obtain water by the arduous but successful method of dropping in a bucket and hauling it up by a rope when full. This then had to be carried to one's individual plot.

Just inside our first plot my father had obtained and installed a fair-sized galvanized tank. The distance from stream to tank must have been about 400 yards. To top up the tank took at least twenty buckets, and he had a big, strong lad who once a week in spring and summer made at least ten journeys to the stream carrying two full buckets of water on the return visit. At least they were full on leaving the stream. I can remember trying a variety of alternative methods of carrying up the water. If I took them on a wheel-barrow the path was so rough that more was spilt than if I carried them by hand. We obtained a barrel such as beer is kept in. I soon discovered why draymen delivering beer bring their dray as close to the cellar flap as possible. The peculiar shape of a beer barrel makes it almost impossible to steer straight. One tended to overfill in order to reduce the number of trips, My strongest recollection of that experiment was that it was more exhausting to roll a barrel full of water than to carry it up two buckets at a time.

No horse's droppings in our neighbourhood escaped the vigilance of our buckets and shovels. I am bound in honesty to admit that my sisters were not excused from this labour. The contents were then conveyed to the allotment and tipped into the galvanised tank. Every time water was added the contents of the tank were stirred and we were left with an evil-smelling but nutritious sludge which could be used to fertilise the allotments as and when required. The consequence was that my father achieved what he dearly wanted, a prize-winning plot with prize-winning soft fruit and vegetables, not only for use at home but – of greater importance – to win prizes at the I.M.M. Flower Shows. So long as I continued to act as principal agricultural labourer at his allotments, relations with my father were strained but tolerable. Brother Chum, in spite of his disability, joined in and my father built up an excellent reputation, winning prizes for his highly productive allotment and for its excellent produce at the annual I.M.M. shows.

One year my father was too ill to do much about the Autumn Show. He always suffered from a weak back. If I remember rightly it had 'gone' completely on this occasion; probably a slipped disc. Chum and I decided that we would use the occasion to demonstrate the extent to which father's reputation was based on our work. So we cosseted marrows, matched giant onions, selected potatoes which were as alike as peas in the pod, and presented as many examples of horticultural excellence as could be imagined. In the event, without my father being able even to attend the show, we won the overall prize for the most awards for our entries. We were thus able to stick a very sharp pin in the balloon of his self-important posturing that success at growing and showing horticultural produce was entirely his own doing.

Thus the days of tension grew to months and the months to years. Political disagreement, educational differences, the non-deferential attitude of the young cub to the old lion, all contributed to the final outburst. One August evening in 1932 I was ordered out of the house. So there I was, homeless, jobless, penniless, on the threshold of beginning a new phase in the journey of my life. Technically I was still a schoolboy, so I rang Chigwell and told the Headmaster that I would not be returning to school in September. "Oh dear!" was his only comment. "I will have to redo my prefects lists".

4

There were no agencies for finding employment for homeless sixteen year old school leavers, regardless of the fact that my three Higher Schools Certificate passes qualified me to apply for a University place. I beat the maggots out of furs in Bread Street; I moved up a bit to become a clerk at William Whiteley's, and lost my job because my revolutionary political ideas and activities became known. Eventually I applied for and got a job in the Works Account department of Mitcham Works, the main U.K. manufacturing centre for the recently amalgamated Phillips and Mullard companies.

Although my job was very junior and incredibly boring I threw myself into the sporting activities sponsored by the company. I became at various times secretary of sections devoted to rifle shooting, table tennis, swimming and darts. Not unnaturally the (paid) secretary of the overall sports club activities was not unattracted to an energetic and educated young employee who was willing to undertake such mundane but necessary tasks as finding out the governing bodies of the various sports and applying for affiliation. It occurred to me that if we were to become one sports club we had better all operate under one name. Up to that point clubs which had operated under the Phillips name before the amalgamation of the companies continued to do so. Similarly with Mullard initiatives. After a great deal of consultation I proposed to the management that a composite name should be adopted for all sports activities and that it should contain the 'ill' from Phillips and the 'ard' from Mullard and, to give it a touch of class, the 'ach' from Achilles. Thus the Achillard sports club was born.

I had borrowed a tandem bicycle from Dr Harold Priestley, chairman of Ilford W.E.A.[13] On this I rode solo every Friday night from Mitcham to Ilford, and back again every Sunday night. I was looking for

---

[13] Workers' Educational Association

a room near the works. A kindly workman, a Mr Tarrant, whose daughter was in the same department as me, made some enquiries and sent me a note to say that he had fixed me up to have a room in the house of the widow of a former colleague. She was named Mrs Gutsole. She was about 58 and had a son Keith, a timid lad who I suspect had a worse time because of his name. Referring obliquely to the fact that I sometimes arrived late on a Sunday night after a weekend visit to Ilford, he wrote: "I have explained to her that you sometimes come late".

It became clear that it would greatly help the integration and growth of the Sports Club if we had a regular magazine. So the Achillard magazine was born at the end of '36. Although the function of the Achillard magazine was mainly to give news, reports and result sequences of club sporting activities, we gradually built up a small but growing number of fictional stories, usually based upon a department of the company or a particularly noteworthy fellow employee.

One day I received a short story written by one of the clever technicians who were working on the development of television. In brief the story purported to tell of a young technician who came back into the T.V. development laboratory to close everything down for the night. To his horror he saw what looked to be a fierce electrically-generated fire burning at the far end of the laboratory. There in front of him was a television screen completely covered, from within, by a fierce white light. From the centre of the screen a sepulchral voice was saying, "I am old Meg of the Wandle. I am here to warn you that you are playing with bad magic. Discontinue your experiments at once or the consequences will be terrible". At which the bright light faded and the T.V. screen cleared to its normal switched-off black state. After checking that all electric plugs were pulled out and that there was no possible danger of fire the technician left.

The story caused some amusement amongst the television researchers and no little credence amongst the less knowledgeable of their fellow workers, so we decided to follow it up with some fictional 'research'. In the next issue we ran the story of an old witch who had lived in a hovel which had once stood on the very spot where the T.V. set of our previous issue was now placed. She had lived beside the river Wandle in the 15th century and had been submitted to the water test for witchcraft. She was strapped to a chair which was lowered into the river until she was submerged. If she drowned, it proved she was a witch receiving just desserts for her activities. If she did *not* drown it proved she was a witch. Only a witch could be submerged on a ducking stool and escape drowning.

Again the imaginative little story achieved some acclaim and was then put out of mind until a few weeks later I received a visit from the editor, and one other, of the Psychic Times. They brought with them copies of their paper in which they had taken quite literally and seriously our little extravaganza about old Meg of the Wandle. They wanted me to get permission from my management for them to exorcise and lay to rest the ghost of old Meg. In their own journal they had really gone to town. It was not often their lot to have authentication and research of the life and death of a 15th century witch written up in a journal which, for the most part, served a very modern and scientific readership. I explained that it was all a fiction. They replied that it couldn't be, as they had written it up in great detail in their journal. I introduced them to the author of the fiction who explained how he had 'made it up as a bit of fun'. They didn't believe him. In the end we had to have them escorted from the premises by our security staff, who were sworn never to let them in again.

* * *

The Workers' Educational Association in Ilford was a splendid example of non-profit-making further education. There were no qualifications for membership. Sex, education and political orientation could not provide a hindrance. Anyone over eighteen could join, although I was given a special dispensation as my Higher School Certificate results normally presupposed an eighteen year old.

The branch in Ilford had membership which belied the name 'workers'. The President was a grammar school headmaster (Dr Harold Priestley, headmaster of Plaistow Grammar School), and most of the regular members were men and women with professional qualifications or university degrees or both. I found their company fascinating. We had regular weekly discussions of topics which were in the news. Terry Farrell, for example, was a fireball member of the British Union of Fascists and did not hesitate to take advantage of the freedom he would deny to others (were he and his party in power), the freedom to challenge and criticise those with whom they disagreed. Victor Smith was a senior inspector of taxes; Kenneth Bloomfield a luminary of the Bank of England; Laurie Cutmore was a solicitor. We had one or two heads of small businesses. On the whole the political atmosphere was slightly left of centre (Blairite?) but discussion was always intelligent and informed.

There were one or two manual workers but I can hardly remember them, except for one council labourer who made timely intercessions in debate. He was called Len Thompson. The W.E.A. not only ran classes but provided a rich and varied social side. Each week we would meet in members' drawing rooms to discuss some matter of current or abstract interest. Every Sunday, weather permitting, we would set off on what in those days we called a 'hike'.

I can remember one Sunday in Epping Forest when we came upon a group of young Germans. Anxious to show a fraternal attitude to foreign visitors we started to sing the Internationale.[14] This was furiously interrupted by a vigorous rendering of the Horst Wessel song. The other party was a Hitler Youth Group, probably learning how to set up a spy cell in Epping.

One Friday evening I went along to a meeting of the W.E.A. Forum, as we called our discussion circle. As I went into the room in which the meeting was to be held I saw a vision of loveliness such as I had never imagined in all my romantic reveries. She was slight, about 5 foot 3 inches, I think, and perfectly formed. She had a beautiful oval face crowned with a head of heavy black curls. But the jewels were her eyes. Oh! Those eyes! Large and round, but of a shining startling blue. For it was love at first sight. Her name was Gwen Pickard. I rapidly discovered that she was at present unattached, a condition that filled me with amazement, and that she would be hiking two days later. I was the

---

[14] *Arise ye starvelings from your slumbers*
Arise ye criminals of want
For reason in revolt now thunders
And at Last ends the age of cant
Now away with all your superstitions,
Servile masses arise arise!
We'll change forthwith the old conditions
And spurn the dust to win the prize!

Then comrades come rally
And the last fight let us face.
The Internationale unites the human race,
Then, comrades, come rally!
And the last fight let us face.
The Internationale unites the human race.

Text: Eugene Pottier (1816-1887)

younger of the two of us, but a six foot, twelve stone athlete. You may be sure I bore myself well throughout our first meetings. She could not have been unaware of my feelings, which must have shone out like a beacon. In quick time we paired up on our Sunday hikes.

Gwen was a wilful young woman. Her looks and her wit combined to ensure that even her more outrageous idiosyncrasies were overlooked or forgiven. For example, each of our Sunday outings had a different leader who was responsible for time of assembly, destination, time and place of stopping for lunch and any other details in the planning of the outing. The time would come when the leader would call a halt at the place selected for the consumption of sandwiches. Everyone would sink to the ground and make themselves comfortable for the lunch break – except Gwen. Completely ignoring the leader's invitation to settle down for lunch she would continue on her way. Because she was young, petite and beautiful her wilfulness would be ignored and the rest of the outing settled in for lunch. After my lightning-strike I could not stand by and see her ignored. Nobody who knew her tried to persuade her. Nobody followed her. Until I did. And found her sometimes less than twenty yards away, so that she would know when the main party moved on. I was still struck, and gradually we got into the habit of lunching separately from the main body.

My recollection, which may have been coloured in a purple glow, was that it was always warm and sunny in those glorious days. But perhaps it was the rain which caused us from time to time to go back to Gwen's house and spend the day looking at the Sunday papers and at one another. Her mother would give us tea. It was here I learnt a solemn lesson. Do not let politeness, or a desire to give a good impression, encourage you to declare enjoyment at some item of food which, frankly, you do not like at all. So it was when one Sunday I was presented with little triangles of 'hammy-cheeses', bland spreading cheese of the type made famous by St Ivel, flavoured with a tiny touch of ham.

"How do you like the hammy-cheese?" asked Mrs Olive. Anxious not to be impolite I expressed great pleasure in the nauseous delicacy. In the next five years I was condemned to hammy-cheeses whenever I had tea with Gwen's mother.

Gwen's stepfather had been very friendly with a neighbour who was a construction engineer. His work, I suspect, was mainly on the drawing board, but his visits to sites involved occasional heavy lifting and moving of prefabricated metal parts. One day he overstrained himself and had a heart attack. When he recovered the doctors told him that he must never again do heavy work. Being still young and needing to continue to earn a living he took a short course on boot and shoe repairing. He and his charming wife moved out of the hustle-bustle of a London suburb and set up in Much Hadham, a small Hertfordshire town, deep in the country. He was a thinking man and soon built up a coterie of visitors who came to his shop not only to have their footwear repaired but also to chat to the man whose intelligence, ready wit and worldly experience gave him the status of village philosopher.

In Ilford he and his wife, who was a merry rosy-cheeked little dumpling of a lady, having no children of their own, became very attracted by Gwen and attached to her as she grew from infancy to womanhood. Not unnaturally they invited her, if ever her Sunday perambulations took her their way, to make a point of calling in. When my relationship with Gwen developed it was inevitable that I should accompany her to visit her friends. We found that he and I had in common a great interest in and affinity to the old Greek philosophers. It was not only Plato and Aristotle whose visions of a perfect society were examined but many of their less well-known contemporaries were recalled with great pleasure. In the meantime Gwen and the lady of the house occupied themselves with more mundane but probably much more useful deliberations. Our growing pleasure in one another's company led to the invitation that we should spend an occasional night in their house whenever we made the journey unaccompanied by our friendly hiking companions. I am talking about seventy years ago so you may be sure that all the conventions were observed. It did, however, throw us even more closely together for longer periods of time, feeding the passion that was growing in us both.

One hot sunny Saturday – we had spent Friday night in our friends' house – we went for a walk in the deserted Hertfordshire countryside. We found a cool and shady thicket beside a narrow and gently flowing stream. I cannot remember whose idea it was that we should strip off to our underclothing and go into the coolness of the stream. When we came out I used my shirt to dab and rub her beautiful body dry. The inevitable followed. We were in love with one another and had been so for over a year. Self control could not last for ever. We each lost our virginity simultaneously in the gentle warmth of a Herfordshire meadow, or was it a copse or a thicket? I do not remember, but I will never forget the ecstasy of the first consummation of our love, nor would I ever want to. Both our Hertfordshire friends and Gwen's mother must have suspected correctly the cause of our changed mien and, to my surprise, both parties – especially Mrs Olive – seemed to welcome and even encourage the growth of our intimacy.

* * *

As a young woman my future mother-in-law had met and made love with a young trainee manager for a Far Eastern Bank. She became pregnant with Gwen. Although the bank's rules forbade marriage under the age of 30, Sidney Pickard did the honourable thing. They were married in 1913, and Gwen was born the following Spring. The other inhibition placed by the bank on its employees was that they were not to volunteer for the Armed Forces without the company's permission. I believe that there was a ballot amongst all bank employees who wished to join up. The two winners would be allowed to go and fight. Sidney was one of the winners. He joined the Army, went to France and was killed at Passchendaele in 1917.

Mrs Olive had, before the outbreak of the 1914 war, been one of the first stenographers to be trained on the new comptometer. She never again went to work but lived on the pensions awarded by the bank and by the War Office. A few years later she married a lonely bachelor she met at the seaside. He was a schoolmaster who taught at the elementary school at which I was a pupil. He had very red hair. His name was Mr Olive, known to everyone, of course, as 'Ginger' Olive. He was a strict teacher, as I remember, who always carried a walking-stick with a long pointed ferrule. This he would use for emphasis or correction by pressing it firmly, point first, into the body or legs of any offender. They married and had in succession a daughter, Audrey and a son, Ralph. One day their father caught meningitis at the swimming pool, became very ill and died. Gwen was left at a very early age with a twice widowed mother and a half brother and half sister.

Into this menage I came a few years after Gwen's grandfather committed suicide. It is impossible to know the reason for his actions. However both his wife, Grandma Speller, and his daughter, Dorothy Olive, were stronger characters than he was. He was a very gentle, kind-hearted, slow-moving horticulturalist who loved country living and his beautiful granddaughter with equal fervour. He left Gwen £100 in his will to be used as she wished after the age of 16. When she reached that age she asked her mother for some of her inheritance. She was presented with a notebook in which a very long list of minor payments had been registered:

Postage stamp	1d	Bus fare	3d
Half yard elastic	7d	Cinema	6d
Notebook	3d	Postage stamp	1d

This went on and on until it added up to over £100. There was no inheritance left for poor Gwen.

The Olive house, 61 Colombo Road, Ilford, was part of a typical suburban terrace, built mainly for the growing numbers of clerical workers and managers who needed easy public transport access to the City of London.

The house had three bedrooms in the main building and a small bedroom down three steps in an annexe built onto the back. I was invited whenever I came to Ilford to use the bedroom in the annexe. As our intimacy grew Gwen would come into my bed for the most tender and passionate of cuddles. I believe her mother was aware all along what what was going on. She clearly encouraged the romance – and fed it on hammy-cheeses. I was not on speaking terms with my father and in those days it was necessary to ask parental permission to get married under the age of twenty-one. I was so much in love with Gwen that I would have done anything to avoid losing her, but I was very surprised when Mrs Olive told me the date of my forthcoming wedding to her daughter. It was to be on the Easter Saturday after my twenty-first birthday (February 15th). So in 1937, still a minor clerk in an office, I became a married man. In case of misunderstanding I must reiterate that although the actual date and arrangements for the wedding were pursued without me being consulted, I went willingly; I would have done anything to avoid losing Gwen. Children followed inevitably and fully desired on both our parts; Anne in 1938 and Susan in 1940.

* * *

War was inevitable against Germany and I, with hundreds of other patriotic and/or anti-Fascist young men joined the Territorial Army. The nearest centre was about a mile and half from the home we set up in a flat in Wallington. The C.O. of my T.A. unit was a Lieutenant Colonel Stuart Ross Moss Vernon. He had been a junior officer in the First World War, and continued his Territorial service after the 1918 Armistice. He was a member of the Moss family who had deep interests in show business, including ownership of the Moss Empire theatres.

Rumour had it that he had been born Vernon Moses but, faced with the anti-Semitism of senior members of the War Office, had reversed his names to become Moss Vernon and acquired a Scottish background by adopting the Christian names of Stuart Ross.

At that time a number of aristocratic and often wealthy young men were joining the T.A. Col. Moss Vernon recruited as many of them as possible to his banner. I well remember the two captains. One of them, a Captain Behrens, was a member of the banking family and his best friend, a Captain Stopford, who had been a student with him at Oxford, had been a member of the Oxford Boat Race crew a few years previously. Most interesting to me was a third class Warrant Officer (Sergeant Major Class III) named Sir Richard Brinsley Ford. He was a lovely man. Tall, cadaverous and unworldly he managed to wear his uniform so badly, through absent-mindedness, that almost every time he went to London the military police would stop him, unable to believe that such an unsoldierly fellow could possible be a Sergeant Major. A Colonel had the power to promote up to the rank of Warrant Officer III. Colonel Moss Vernon could not bear to have our hereditary nobleman in the lower ranks, so Sir Richard was recommended for training as an officer. He was not accepted. So he was recommended for promotion to Warrant Officer Class I or II. He was not accepted, not surprisingly, for he was the most unmilitary man I ever met, albeit one of the most charming.

We were a searchlight unit. When war broke out we were stationed in Surrey on the route from the South Coast of England to London. I well remember Richard coming to me in the middle of a dark, dark night. All one could see were searchlights either pointing towards the sea and slowly moving towards London or vice versa. I was then a newly promoted 2nd Lieutenant in charge of a sector of the sky.

"Sir," said Sir Richard. "All we seem to be doing is showing the buggers coming in the location of the buggers going out. Would it not be more helpful if we all switched off our searchlights simultaneously? With luck they might collide with one another."

On another occasion we were paraded to hear a lecture on Greece. There was currently news about gallant guerrilla activity by Greek patriots resisting German occupation, so there was a full house. It turned out that two Cambridge botany dons had just before the war returned from a plant gathering mission in Greece. They had kindly volunteered to go round Army units giving a lecture on their experiences. One of them with, in the circumstances, the unfortunate name of Dr

Balls, referred to the kindness of the Greek Ministry of Agriculture who had lent them an expert on Greek plants to help their research. He referred to the Minister by name. At which point Sergeant Major Ford, who had a marvellous languid upper class voice, interrupted; could he ask a question?

"Of course", said the lecturer.

"Did you say, Sir", drawled Sir Richard, "That his name was *Oino*kopolous or *Oiko*nopolous?"

I think he was deadly serious but to this day I have the feeling that Sir Richard was the only person in the room who had the courage to show his boredom.

The National Service call-up had created an urgent call for officers. Of the ten members of my searchlight unit, seven or eight were sent to officer training units. I went to the O.C.T.U.[15] at Shrivenham in Wiltshire. We were sent off in batches in alphabetical order. I can remember we went from LUMB to MULLIGAN in the barrack room where I slept. Getting to know one another in barracks for the most part consisted of anecdotal accounts of where men had come from and the characteristics of the people amongst whom they had been stationed. At one point the discussion ranged about relative standards of hospitality. A Scottish cadet, McDiarmid, had said nothing, but lay back on his bunk smoking. Suddenly he sat up.

"Ye ken nothing about hospitality", he said. "There was a commercial traveller in the Highlands of Scotland forced off the road by torrential rainfall. He called at a cottage and asked if he could come in, dry his clothes and perhaps stay the night. He was made welcome and served a splendid hot meal brought to his table by a most attractive young woman.

"The rains stopped; the clouds cleared and, under a bright full moon, it looked very appealing outdoors. With his eye on the main chance the traveller, English of course, invited the young woman, the daughter of the house, to accompany him on a short stroll in the field beyond the house. He persuaded her to sit down on the ground. Then to lie down. Suddenly he was alarmed to hear a window flung open in the house, and a solicitous voice call:

"Muareg. Muareg. Arch your back a wee bit and keep the gentleman's balls off the wet grass".

---

[15] Officer Cadet Training Unit

"That", said McDiarmid, "is hospitality".

* * *

So we progressed slowly through the next two years. My own two lives were parallel but hardly seemed to touch. On the domestic front we moved into a charming little bungalow off the main road in Wallington. Our next door neighbours became close friends. Laurie Dickenson was a window dresser in Gamages in High Holborn. From time to time he would overcome his boredom by displaying nonsense or even slightly rude notices in the window. One day he went too far for the rather Victorian-minded management. He was sacked. In revenge his last act as an employee was to plaster the windows with placards which read: 'Bargain. Not to be repeated. Miscarriages rewheeled'. A crowd assembled outside the shop. Many people, after goggling at the notices, went in and made purchases. Overcoming their prudish objections – remember, this is about 1938 – the management withdrew their dismissal notice and reinstated him at an increase in salary.

When the time came for him to be called up he went into the infantry as a private soldier. His regiment was posted to Scotland to mount guard on public buildings in case of a German invasion. This suggested to Laurie a splendid new hobby. He would collect the main door keys of as many important buildings as possible. He did not survive the war, but his widow proudly showed me his collection, pride of place being the enormous key to Stirling Castle. Emily was a rosy-cheeked, middle-aged lady who had no children and who became very attached to my little ones. She frequently gave herself respite from the bombing in London when I moved my family to Grantham some years later. There, by coincidence, the grocer with whom we were registered was Alderman Roberts, father of Margaret Thatcher. Anne shared with her the honour of being a pupil of Kesteven and Grantham Grammar school – but not, of course, at the same time.

In July 1939 we went into summer camp at Edenbridge in Kent. By mid-August war became inevitable and we were kept mobilised, becoming fully part of the Air Defence of Great Britain when war was officially declared in September. Many of my T.A. colleagues were recommended for commissions. I was sent to the Officer Cadet Training Unit at Shrivenham in Wiltshire, from which I emerged in 1939 as a 2nd Lieutenant in the Royal Artillery.

5

My career as a subaltern officer in Air Defence was brief. I had six searchlight sites which I had the responsibility to command and train. Fortunately each site had an experienced sergeant who knew more precisely than I ever would the drills for operating searchlights.

The saddest duty I had to perform was the weekly pay parade. I can remember one soldier who was married with a child and had to give part of his pay to his wife. Alas he also had a mistress with a court order distraining most of what was left of his pay. One week he had an unfortunate incident with a can of lighter fuel and burnt a hole in his uniform, for the repair of which he had to pay. So Gunner Lewington came on pay parade, his name was called and the amount of his entitlement – sixpence – was announced. He came forward, received his meagre pittance and spun it contemptuously in the air before catching it and putting it into his pocket. The sergeant in charge of the pay parade immediately put him under arrest, I think for carrying out a bit of drill that was not in the manual. As soon as the pay parade was over approximately the same personnel were assembled to try the villainous Lewington. He was, of course, guilty and I had to sentence him. I ordered the sergeant to withdraw and I put a shilling on the table which I said Lewington must have dropped. Without batting an eyelid he saluted, picked up the shilling and smartly did an about turn and marched off.

Another character who I will never forget was a 24 stone six foot eight inch professional all-in wrestler named Bombadier Baltus. He was a gentle giant with an extraordinarily high pitched voice. He first came to my notice one day when I was orderly officer. Central to the morning and evening parades were the raising and lowering of the Union Jack. On this occasion a high wind had spun the ropes at the top of the flagpole into a tangle which could not be released from the ground. I was told of a small conscript who had been a merchant seaman. He assured me that he could shin up the pole. Two thirds of the way up, and the top of the pole was swinging backwards and forwards dangerously. The ex-sailor slid down rapidly and withdrew his volunteered offer to go to the top and disentangle the ropes. At this point Baltus appeared. Clutching the flagpole against his chest he managed to wriggle it loose in its hole. Gradually he lifted it vertically out of its seating and, with a mighty effort, lifted it completely out of the ground and laid it gently down. It was a prodigious feat of strength, especially in the face of a near-hurricane wind.

We were stationed near St. Neots. There was only one public house near our tented camp which naturally was frequented whenever off-duty by my lads. One day another unit came into the neighbourhood. They immediately sought to take over the pub. They were led by an energetic Cockney sergeant who challenged anybody who offended him, perhaps by being in front of him in the queue for the bar, by draining his glass of the last drops of beer and inverting it in a challenging way on the bar in front of the nearest 'enemy' soldier. There were one or two fights which my callow young National Service boys lost. So I sent for Bombadier Baltus.

"We're going to the pub this evening, Bombadier, and I am going to buy you a drink".

"But I'm a teetotaller, Sir", he said. "I don't frequent pubs".

"I respect that. What I want you to do is to stop a civil war. Go early to the pub. Find a seat where you can see into the Saloon Bar. I will send you a glass of orange squash. All I want you to do when I signal is to get up out of your seat very slowly and gradually stand up to your full height". In due course the belligerent Sergeant walked in, drained his pint, looked round and saw this bombadier quietly sipping orange squash. The sergeant drained his glass and inverted it in front of Baltus. I signalled. Six foot eight of powerful, strongly muscled bombadier slowly uncoiled himself and equally slowly got to his feet and raised himself to his full height. The sergeant gave one horrified look, left the pub and never again challenged any of my troops.

My final recollection of my short stay as a 2nd Lieutenant in Home Defence concerns General Sir 'Tim' Pile, commander in chief of the Home Defence. We were told on the telephone that General Pile would be spending the night at Brigade Headquarters near Cambridge, and that he would be going past our little camp at 11 a.m. the next day. "The General", we were told, "never passes one of his small units without paying an unannounced visit. So keep your chaps up all night if necessary polishing and bullshitting[16] the camp so that it will look as though you are always as smart as that. Have everyone in their best uniforms – by chance on parade – at 11 o'clock so that you can give him a grand general salute."

So we painted the coal bunkers white, raised the generators on to 'elephant feet' and carefully divided the tyres into seven sections, each marked with the day of the week, so that "they can be rotated daily, Sir, giving the same exposure to the sun to each in turn." A load of bull, of course: the tyres had never been rotated. Came 11 a.m. the next day. Everything spick and span. My little troop just happened to be in their best uniforms on parade, with a keen-eyed lookout to let us know if a staff car was in sight. By midday nobody had dared move in case boots got dusty. I rang Brigade H.Q.

"He's still here", they replied, "but will be along shortly".

At one o'clock the troops went off parade in ones and twos to have something to eat. I rang Brigade H.Q, again. "Yes. He is still coming."

At one thirty I went into my tent, which served also as my office. From out of the News of the World and draped across the typewriter was an advertisement for Germolene with the caption: 'NO TRACE OF PILES'. Years later I sat next to General Pile at a dinner. He was delighted with the story, and made voluminous notes on the back of a menu.

* * *

Towards the end of 1939 I was released from the tedium of my searchlight duties by an Army Council Instruction. The hierarchy of the services – Navy at number one, Army number two and R.A.F. number three – forbade the transfer from a more junior service to one more senior, but it was permissible to seek to recruit officers for transfer to a more junior service. Army Council Instruction 1529 was, therefore, fully in order. It invited young Army officers of the appropriate fitness standards to volunteer for flying training with the R.A.F. If they succeeded in passing the elementary flying standards they obtained their 'wings', a symbolic cloth representation of a bird's wings, which could be

---

[16] Bullshitting – taking exaggerated and unnecessary care in cleaning uniform or barracks to impress senior officers.

sewn on to the left breast of their uniforms.

Opinion has been expressed that in some cases Colonels were delighted to persuade madcap young subalterns to volunteer for training. One thing was certain. The proportion of Army officer volunteers who failed flying training was significantly higher than that of young men, disproportionately from public and grammar schools, who came into training direct from civvy street. Qualified pilots obtained the same basic pay as their equivalent ranks in the Army, plus a generous allowance called Flying Pay. This, coupled with the fact that the R.A.F. was expanding rapidly and that promotion possibilities were good, won me over. I volunteered. My decision was reinforced by Gwen's oldest friend, Hilda Butterworth. They had been together from the age of 10. For no other reason than that I reciprocated heartily Hilda really disliked me, and took every opportunity to reduce me in Gwen's eyes.

"It is disgraceful", she said, not once but many, many times, "for a married man with a child to volunteer for a dangerous occupation like flying military aircraft. *My* husband", she would continue smugly, "has just been accepted as a sergeant in the Education Corps. He will never have to face an enemy and never serve abroad. That is responsible behaviour."

Her intervention was the last argument I needed. I volunteered at the earliest opportunity. I was posted for training with a group of other Army officers and billeted in Selwyn College, Cambridge where there was later a scandal which led to some prosecutions and imprisonment. College servants were appalled that R.A.F. aircrew rations, especially of such luxuries as butter and sugar, were vastly superior to civilian rations. So they stole them and sold them on the black market. This racket had an effect on what was available for the Army officer trainees. Mr Churchill had just made his historic observation:

"Never in the history of human endeavour have so many owed so much to so few".

Inspired by this, one Army Lieutenant – Lieutenant Pink – endorsed his first mess cheque: 'Never in the history of human endeavour have so many paid so much for so little.' He was court-martialled for publishing – in that anyone in the bank could read what he had written – observations which would bring the Army into disrepute. He probably got a black mark on his records, but it initiated an investigation which led to far more serious consequences for some of the Selwyn catering staff. (Incidentally, is it not ironic that Selwyn College,

Cambridge, was a leading theological college at which many Church of England clergy were trained?)

After about six weeks basic training, most of which was familiar to Army officers but which included an introduction to the Theory of Flight, we then went off to Marshall's Airfield, Cambridge to begin our own flying training. The instrument of my training was the wonderful Tiger Moth, a small light bi-plane which was safe, infinitely manoeuvrable and infinitely exciting. My first flying tutor was a tough-looking but beautifully spoken sergeant-pilot named David Balme. I was an Army Lieutenant and, without undue deference or obsequiousness, he observed the decencies due to my senior rank, but really due to him because of his vastly superior skill. One day, flying locally around and over Cambridge I said to David, "You are the first instructor, Army or Air force, who in the process of getting acquainted failed to ask your pupil what he did before he joined up."

"That is because when they have answered, they always say, 'And what did you do?'"

"If it's such a mystery, Sergeant – tell me, what did you do?"

He leaned over the side of the aircraft, pointed downwards, and said, "I taught Greek and Latin in that university."

He was a Cambridge don with a fierce sense that war against German Nazism called for the maximum personal effort from all good men and true. He had volunteered for the R.A.F. and the powers-that-be had arrived at the brilliant conclusion that an Oxbridge Classics don's future in the R.A.F. was best served as a teacher of elementary flying. He was always in trouble. It was natural for him to meet his former students and stand about, jacket unbuttoned, hands in trouser pockets, discussing whatever is discussed by dons and students in a major university town. The military police frankly did not like it. To them he was not a don. He was an R.A.F. sergeant dressed disgracefully. He was continually on a 'charge', until he was rescued by the granting of his oft-repeated request for a posting to a Bomber training unit.

Life is full of interesting coincidences. I got to know my sergeant instructor quite well in the few weeks it took to get me through the rudiments of flying a Tiger Moth. He had a messianic desire to become a heavy bomber pilot, and to go to war against Nazi Germany. I lost sight of David for about five years. Then when I was elected to a seat in the House of Commons I handed over 227 Squadron to the command of Wing Commander David Balme D.S.O., D.F.C., a distinguished bomber ace coming back for a further term of operational flying.

* * *

Meanwhile, like many other service wives, Gwen was having a hard time. At first money had been desperately short. I cannot remember exactly what my pay and her marriage allowance came to, but it was very little. The Bank of England would no longer employ her, because it was not policy to employ married women. She was able to get modest clerical employment locally, but full-time childcare was expensive and in one case turned out to be positively against the best interests of Anne, our first-born.[17] Then there was the added risk of living close to Croydon airport. It now served a completely military purpose and there were clear signs that it would be targeted for bombing by the Luftwaffe. Which meant that nobody within a radius of a mile of Croydon aerodrome was safe. So we found a tiny but inexpensive cottage to rent in a little village in Northamptonshire called Melchbourne. Melchbourne was really only a single row of cottages leading to a church, with one shop which also served as the village Post Office. It was, I suspect, desperately boring for Gwen and Anne, but it was safe. They rented a cottage from a family called Hales. The village was about ten miles from Cambridge.

When I was learning to fly, David Balme suggested that we could easily fly over to Melchbourne and drop a message to my wife. So I wrote a loving note, wrapped it up with a heavy stone in a handkerchief, and made another handkerchief into a parachute. We duly flew the few miles to Melchbourne and, coming down low, circled the church spire. Villagers appeared and waved. We waved back and dropped the parachute message. Eventually, having exchanged several minutes of friendly greeting we flew back to base. Two days later I received a furious letter from Gwen. We had arrived on a Sunday evening. The whole village was in church. We appeared overhead just as the vicar was beginning his sermon. When we did not go away, but continued to roar at low level round the church, they all came out, waved their fists and shouted for us to go away. Of course, we could not hear. All we could see was a crowd of villagers waving enthusiastically.

Although Gwen didn't stay very long in Melchbourne it was

---

[17] We discovered that Anne was left on a pot sometimes for two to three hours at a time and punished if she got off.

followed by a strange coincidence many years later. We were on holiday in America, staying in a small town in Pennsylvania. Our host told us that there was an elderly immigrant of British origin who loved to meet visitors from the U.K. Would we like to meet him? Of course we would. We were taken along to a small but charming house with a ladder up one side. At the top of the ladder was an elderly man doing repairs to the roof or gutter. He came down, and we asked him where in England he came from.

"You would never have heard of it," he said. "It's a tiny hamlet near Rushden called Melchbourne." It turned out that his name was Bill Hales, and that he was born in the very cottage where Gwen and Anne had stayed in 1940.

By early summer 1940 I had been awarded my 'wings'. Since I had not yet been transferred to the R.A.F. I sewed my wings on to my Army tunic. I went about in the strange mixture of R.A.F. insignia on an Army uniform. It led to some interesting misunderstandings. About that time parachute training had started in the Army. I must, therefore, have been specially selected to be trained by the R.A.F. in the new skill of military parachute dropping. Some people thought I was a special agent serving the needs of the Army and the R.A.F. To others I must have been a German spy who had his uniforms muddled. Needless to say, I enjoyed the mystery. To have sought to explain would have been tedious. And no fun.

Eventually my transfer to the R.A.F. came through and I became a fully qualified Pilot Officer in the R.A.F. Although I had been obliged to drop a rank, the award of flying pay actually gave me a small rise in income. Possibly because of my age, I was selected for training as a flying instructor and was posted to Montrose to be prepared for this important and highly dangerous occupation. At Montrose we shared the military honour with a small naval unit. Equipped with requisitioned coastal fishing boats they plied up and down the coast keeping vigilance against unauthorised intruders and performing such menial tasks as finding and marking any buoys which had got loose and were drifting aimlessly along the coast to the danger of naval and civilian shipping. Most of the crew were in fact local fishermen who had only recently been called up. Not unnaturally, because their military task was not very taxing, they spent a lot of time fishing. We soon discovered that they had the privilege, which they exercised, of being allowed to buy duty-free spirits, but they received desperately meagre food rations. We made friends. It was very pleasant to provide, through our Officers Mess, a joint of meat in lieu of the meals they missed because they spent as much time afloat as possible, in return for gin or whisky.

I received my qualification as a flying instructor and was posted to R.A.F. Spitalgate, just outside Grantham. Although we worked long duty hours, married officers were permitted to live out with their families. We rented an old Victorian house in Castlegate, a road honoured by having at one end the grocer's shop of the Mayor, Alderman Roberts, father of Margaret Thatcher, and at the other Kesteven and Grantham Girls Grammar School. It was pleasant living out with my wife and family. By this time we had two daughters, Anne and Susan. Here it was that I developed a taste and no small expertise in making up and recounting stories for children. The technique was simple, but much enjoyed by the young. I took a well-known story such as Cinderella and developed the story with one or more of the children playing an active role in it.

By a happy coincidence my youngest daughter Caroline, who has been an enormous help and encouragement to me in developing the writing of my life story, found and sent me an old, old copy of 'Teddy's Adventures' which illustrates the story-telling technique and more than hints at the pleasure given in the writing and listening.

Teddy's Adventures[18]

Chapter I

Outside all was quiet. A kindly moon was smiling down on a still, peaceful world. Just outside a pretty village on the banks of a great river stood the house. Ringed round by great trees and with a lawn surrounded by beds in which many flowers hung their heads sleepily, the house too was still and at rest.

Inside Mummy and Daddy were asleep in their bedroom. In the next room Caroline, a pretty little girl with fair curly hair and blue eyes, lay asleep in her own blue bed. Beside her, stiff and staring, sat Teddy, her white toy bear. Nothing stirred except the gentle sighing of the wind in the trees outside and the rhythmic tick-tock of the clock on Caroline's mantelpiece. Suddenly, with an important whirring of tiny wheels, the clock chimed the quarters and struck twelve times. It was midnight.

---

[18] Written in the early 1950s

"Goodness me", said Teddy, grumpily, as he stretched his arms and legs,"how long one has to wait nowadays for midnight to strike. It seems a very nice evening, I think I'll call on the dolls in the nursery and take them out for a stroll."

As he turned quietly over he noticed that his movements were being watched by Caroline who had opened one bright blue eye. "Wait for me, Teddy" whispered Caroline, "I'm coming too".

"Oh all right" he replied "but be very quiet. If you waken Mummy or Daddy I will have to go stiff again until tomorrow night, and that will spoil everything".

So very quietly they both got up and dressed, Caroline in her white jumper, jeans and sandals, and Teddy in grey knickers, a red and white striped Tee shirt and red dancing shoes.

Hand in hand they crept quietly downstairs, being especially careful as they passed the stair that squeaked.

When they reached the nursery they found all the dolls and soft animals moving about talking and giggling.

"Quiet, everybody" said Teddy, in a gruffety kind of voice, "Caroline and I are going to take you for a walk if you are good. As it is a nice night I think we will take a picnic".

"I'll cut the sandwiches" said Elizabeth, the fair haired teenage doll, who really belonged to Caroline's sister, Deborah.

"I'll make some tea and fill a thermos flask" said Waggles, the toy dog and oldest member of the nursery.

In less time than it takes to say 'Cheese and Biscuits' a lovely picnic had been prepared and packed up and all was ready for the night's fun.

Chapter II

They had decided to make their picnic down by the great river. Their way led alongside a high wall. As they were passing, all skipping or jumping and enjoying every minute, except for Teddy who was importantly holding the picnic basket. Caroline suddenly looked up, "Oh what a funny looking creature" she cried pointing up to the top of the wall.

"Funny looking creature yourself" said a shrill voice. "Don't you know it's rude to point? What's your name?"

Everybody stopped and looked up. There balanced on the top of the wall was a roundy-poundy creature with no hair and a wide smile. He wore a little scarlet jacket, green trousers, yellow shoes and an enormous cravat in black and white check.

"I'm Caroline, and I'm sorry if I sounded rude but you did give me a surprise. This is Teddy and these are all my dolls and animals. Who are you?"

"Who am I?" mimicked the roundy-poundy creature, "Why, I'm Humpty Dumpty, who else sits on a wall?"

As he spoke, Humpty Dumpty started to rock backwards and forwards, smiling broadly and humming cheerfully to himself.

"Oh do be careful, sir" growled Teddy, "you'll fall off if you rock backwards and forwards like that".

"Rubbish", said Humpty Dumpty, "I'll not fall off" and he began to hum more loudly and to rock backwards and forwards more violently.

"Oh dear! Look out!" cried Caroline, but it was too late. Humpty Dumpty toppled right off the wall and Splish! Splash! Splosh! fell into one hundred thousand pieces, all over the path and the pavement.

Chapter III

"Oh dear! Teddy, whatever shall we do?" cried Caroline.

"You go that way and I'll go this way" said Teddy "and look for help".

So followed by dolls and animals they ran off in opposite directions until Caroline saw coming towards her one of the King's Men, looking very smart indeed in a new uniform and riding one of the King's Horses.

"Hello, Caroline", he said, saluting smartly when he saw Caroline running towards him.

"Is anything the matter?"

"Please come at once", said Caroline, "Humpty Dumpty has rocked backwards and forwards too hard and fallen Splish, Splash, Splosh off the wall and broken into one hundred thousand pieces all over the path and the pavement".

"Don't you worry, Miss" said the King's Man. "I'll just dash off and fetch all the King's Horses and all the King's Men."

Caroline and the dolls went back to where Humpty Dumpty lay smashed all over the road whilst one of her bunnies who could run very fast went off to fetch back Teddy and the dolls who had gone with him.

In less than two minutes there came a great galloping and up rode all the King's Horses and all the King's Men, some carrying dustpans and brushes, some string, some sticky paper and some pots of glue.

They set to work, some brushing, some tying, some sticking and some gluing and in less than no time they *could* put Humpty Dumpty together again. And they did.

Chapter IV

When Humpty Dumpty was put together again and the King's Horses had galloped off with the King's Men – who had been warmly thanked by Caroline and Teddy for the wonderful rescue – Teddy said "Not much time left for our picnic, let's go into this field and have our feast."

So they went into a field, accompanied by Humpty Dumpty and ate sandwiches and jelly and cream, tea out of dollys' cups, two kinds of cake and ice cream.

When tea was over and everything packed up they played all kinds of games. Teddy was blindfolded first when they played Blind Man's Buff. Caroline was first at Sally in the Middle. They all danced the polka. Then Humpty Dumpty sang a special song about falling off the wall and being rescued by all the King's Horses and all the King's Men.

Suddenly in the distance they heard a cockerel crow "Cock-a-doodle-doo".

"Bless my furry paws", gasped Teddy, "We'll have to hurry back if we're to get indoors again before daylight. Come on everyone, home quickly".

With a great scampering and scurrying the dolls packed up the picnic things and ran breathlessly all the way back to the house.

Caroline and Teddy saw all the dolls and animals back into the nursery.

"Goodnight, everybody" they said "thank you for a lovely adventure".

"Goodnight Caroline". "Goodnight Teddy" called the dolls and animals.

Quickly and quietly Teddy and Caroline crept upstairs again, being specially careful as they passed the stair that creaked.

"Goodnight Teddy" said Caroline as she slipped into her little blue bed. But Teddy was already stiff and glassy eyed, staring into nothingness and dreaming of his night's activities.

With a contented smile Caroline turned over and had only just dropped off to sleep when she heard Mummy's voice saying "Come along, Caroline darling, time to get up".

And the next day had begun.

6

Perhaps the most important thing about teaching is that one is compelled to master one's subject if one wants to teach effectively. Demonstrations must be as nearly perfect as possible and only a mastery of the subject enables an authoritative answer to the questions one expects good students to raise. So I began an invaluable year in Flying Training Command, learning how to perform the basics of flying. Learning *why* they are the basics. Making mistakes. Working out what went wrong. Learning how to correct mistakes.

Flying is a fantastic activity. It engenders a wonderful spirit of mastery and freedom. Woe betide any pilot, however experienced, who forgets that an aeroplane is balanced on a column of that most fragile of elements, air. Because of the thrill implicit in flying and because the authorities want combat pilots to be careful but carefree, and since in my day – and I'm sure still – all aircrew recruitment in the R.A.F. is on a volunteer basis, the main source of recruitment is amongst the young, often straight from school. It is in the nature of the young male that by far the majority of the volunteers wanted to become fighter pilots. Preferably of Spitfires. It is also in their nature that they are impatient to get on with the task of flying and give somewhat less of their energy and enthusiasm to an understanding of what forces make an aircraft fly.

I can remember being on a bombing mission to an industrial/military target in South-West France. The meteorologists forecast complete cover of the whole route, until about 20 miles before the target, with the aviator's worst natural enemy, dense cumulus cloud. Inside the cloud, high winds suddenly manifest themselves, vertically, horizontally or even in a mixture of directions. It resembles the itinerary of a corkscrew. On this occasion I had with me in my squadron eleven other pilots. They were all young and in high spirits. The journey out was full of danger. Our bomb and fuel-laden aircraft were too heavy for us to fly over the top; we could not manage the increased altitude. Vigilance had to be of the highest. There was a real danger of collision with twelve aircraft shrouded in a thick white fog, all proceeding in the same direction.

Precisely as briefed, we came to the edge of the thick cloud. There, straight ahead, illuminated by a bright, unclouded sun, lay the target. With great pride I watched the aircraft one after another break out of the thick white wall of cloud. All twelve aircraft dropped their bombs and signalled 'mission successful'. Then, having come through between three and four hours of very, very difficult flying, we had to turn back and make the reciprocal journey. Four aircraft failed to get home safely. Twenty eight brave young men, who had completed their mission, died in the struggle against the elements. One can have many ideas about why they failed. They were not physically mature enough? They had not had sufficient experience of flying under such adverse conditions? They had failed to understand all the hazards of such a trip? Some may even have panicked and lost control. Whatever the actual reasons, they shouldn't have been there. The politics of war, their minimal training, their callowness – all combined to bring about a sad sacrifice.

Reverting to flying training, I well remember an incident in which I was in the wrong. We were flying from an auxiliary airfield called Harlaxton. It was L shaped. Normally one took off and landed along the long body of the L. I was testing aircraft prior to night flying training. The administrative part of the exercise was being carried out at the end of the short side of the L. There was an aircraft ready to test for that night's training at the toe of the short side. Just as I was about to taxi out and take off some airmen, who had discovered that one of their members had never been up in an aircraft, came over and asked me to take their colleague up for his first flight.

"You'll be all right with him", they told the very reluctant virgin passenger. "He's the safest pilot on the station."

By this time it was getting towards dusk, and I was anxious to get airborne as soon as possible. There was further delay while the airman was strapped in. I decided that with a bit of imaginative flying skill I could take off across the toe of the L, instead of spending time taxiing round to the appropriate take-off point. Aiming at the hedge, which was perhaps fifty yards too close for safety, I opened the throttle. As the hedge loomed nearer I pulled back the control column and selected 'Up' on the undercarriage lever.

Just before taking off we hit a bit of very rough ground. Unfortunately the undercarriage was unlocked and the violent impact caused the legs of the undercarriage to bend unnaturally. Not unexpectedly when we got safely airborne the undercarriage would neither come fully up nor down again. I carried out my air test, including the unusual one of diving vertically downwards and then pulling the aircraft into an immediate and violent climb. In theory this should force the undercarriage down into a locked position. Unfortunately the leg was too bent, so I called up the servicing department to say I was bringing her in with the undercarriage so damaged that I would have to land with the wheels unlocked. The manoeuvre was duly carried out and we approached the maintenance area. In the comparative quiet of cutting the engines before the final touch-down I saw my passenger's hands shakily reaching out.

"Does it always catch fire, Sir?" came a frightened little voice.

Of course it did not and the service department took it immediately in hand. I enquired the next day about the well-being of my passenger. He was unhurt, I was told, but had been given a day off to recover from the shock. He swore that he would never go up in an aircraft again.

Our main training at that time was to convert to twin enginned aircraft pilots trained on aircraft with one engine. They had been selected for training ultimately to become night fighter pilots. Their operational aircraft eventually would be Beaufighters, and we began the transition by converting them to the Blenheim 1. Of its family of aircraft the Blenheim 1 was a jewel to fly. It was a twin-engined monoplane which had performed admirable service both as a fighter and as a light bomber. As the technical advances in aircraft design produced planes which were faster and stronger, the Blenheim became outflown and outgunned by its German equivalents. Before it was decided to take it off operational flying there were many disastrous sorties involving heavy losses of aircraft and flying personnel. It made, however, a splendid training aircraft, especially for pilots selected to go on to its big brother, the night-fighter Beaufighter.

Amongst the stream of pilots who had learnt on single-engined aircraft were a number who had been trained in the United States of America. It was a great shock to many to discover that where-ever you are in the United Kingdom, if you fly in a straight line either east or west you are out of the country in not much time. If you went out of the country to the east you were soon over the North Sea. That way lay the enemy. Some pilots who had been trained in America rejoiced in the proximity of danger. I had two Australian pilots. P.O.[19] Cole was a bank clerk from Melbourne before volunteering for the R.A.A.F.[20] His best friend, P.O. Scherf, was a sheep farmer from up country. We discovered that whenever they could each get an aircraft for 'local flying' practice they would meet up and fly east in the hope of seeing a German aircraft.

On the other hand there were those who were amazed there was such a condition as a 'black-out'. They had been accustomed during their training to seeing towns with all lights on. If they got slightly lost they might find the name of the town written in large letters on a gas-holder. There were many other opportunities to discover where they were. Some had been trained in the 'sunshine states' where one could more or less rely on ten consecutive hours of good, clear weather on most days. They came to England. England was small. Security on the ground was designed to make it difficult, if not impossible, for aviators to spot easily where they were. This included those trained in America. But above all there was the English weather. Protracted periods of clear, sunny skies were a rarety. One had to find out how to fly below menacing dark clouds or in violent storms of rain. Especially near industrial towns one frequently found oneself in white or, worse, black fog. These were hazards that one had to learn to overcome if one was to become an operational pilot working out of England.

Some, like my friends Cole and Scherf, greeted the conditions as a challenge. The last I heard of them was that they had managed to keep together and had both performed gallantly and safely in Mosquitos as armed intruders, penetrating well into enemy territory on special missions. Their targets included individual factories of special importance, railway junctions and occasional tank concentrations or other military targets. I am happy to report, as I later discovered, that they had both been posted back to Australia at a time when 'the yellow peril' was a real threat. But because flying conditions for training were so favourable in the United States the end-of-course casualties were often much higher than we suspected they might have been had they been at home. American categories were also slightly different from ours. We normally had Average, Above Average and Below Average. At our training stage nobody was rated Above Average, and anybody Below

---

[19] Pilot Officer

[20] Royal Australian Air Force

Average was taken off flying. The Americans had a category which they called Superior. One or two of the bright young men trained in the States took this categorisation seriously. It was therefore a very difficult job with some to teach them to fly a twin-engined aircraft, to fly in non-Californian weather and to find their way safely round blacked-out countryside.

The two most difficult manoeuvres one has to master when learning to fly are the take-off and the landing. A lot of time is spent, when converting pilots to a new aircraft, in teaching how to line up for a landing, how to reduce speed progressively whilst maintaining full control, when to cut the throttle to allow the aircraft to settle and to run to a halt on the ground. Similarly one teaches how to line up for a straight take-off; the correct speed to pull back the control column to effect safe lift-off; when to retract the undercarriage by engaging the appropriate lever; when to take in the flaps – the adjustable working surfaces on the backs of the wings which, in effect, can increase or diminish the area of the wings – and hence the lift being exerted by the plane.

When one has made sufficient progress with a pupil pilot in the skills of take-off and landing one can shorten the time between practising the separate skills by 'overshooting' – coming right down to just above the ground then opening up the throttle as though one were first taking off. The danger in the overshoot procedure lies in the risk of an engine failure. If one is in a single engined aircraft and the engine cuts out one has the task of finding straight ahead an appropriate landing place. With a twin-engined aircraft the effect of an engine cut on landing, or on practising overshoot procedure, is much more dramatic. The good engine will drive the aircraft away from it. Uncorrected, the plane will lift on the side of the good engine and even flip over on to its back. Corrective action must be taken immediately.

One day I had been doing an intensive series of practice take-offs and landings with a young pilot who had trained in America. He had arrived with a category of 'Superior', which he took seriously, the arrogant little sod! We were in a Blenheim 1, a gentlemanly twin-engined aircraft. All was going well. The pupil-pilot had mastered landings and take-offs fairly well and we were finishing the session with a couple of overshoots. At about 500 feet, overshooting after a simulated landing, the port engine cut and the aircraft began to veer violently to the left. To my amazement and chagrin, instead of trying to regain control of the aircraft the pupil unfastened his safety-belt, opened the window and started to try to climb out. The aircraft had no dual control so I was standing beside the pilot's seat. Simultaneously and immediately it was necessary to turn the control column completely to the right and to try to reach out and stamp on the right rudder pedal, whilst at the same time use my left hand to restrain the idiot who, if he had managed to get out, would undoubtedly have crashed to his death. Neither then nor now have I the faintest idea of how I managed to obtain some slight measure of control of the situation. I know I hit him as hard as I could and managed to pull him off his seat and into the standing room which I was already occupying, with one foot firmly pressed on the right rudder pedal. I would not be here writing this now if I had not been able with an almost superhuman effort to get into the seat and carry out the procedure for engine cut on overshoot in a light twin-engined aircraft. Once obtaining control I then had to contact Flying Control and explain that I had to make a right hand circuit followed by a single-engined landing. The circuit was cleared. I made the appropriate landing. I reported the incident in full and endorsed my report on the 'Superior' student: 'Unfit in temperament or ability to fly multi-engined aircraft'. A few days later I was summoned to report to Wing Commander Abbott, the Wing Commander Flying, and to bring my log book.

"Oh good", I thought, "He is going to write something in my logbook about the overshoot incident". Not a bit of it.

"I have seen the report of the careless way in which you wrecked the undercarriage of an aircraft you should have been testing for night flying".

"Before you do that, sir", I interrupted. "Have you seen the report of the overshoot incident which occurred yesterday?"

"Oh, that", he replied, with a shrug. "Quite interesting, if true".

I was livid. This, coming from a man designated Wing Commander Flying who nobody could every remember seeing flying an aircraft.

"If you propose giving me a red endorsement for careless flying I shall write to the A.O.C.[21] requesting consideration for a green endorsement at least for saving two lives and an aircraft".

"You cannot write to the A.O.C. except with my permission".

---

[21] Air Officer Commanding

"Oh yes I can. The Air Council Instruction is specific that the rule can be waived if the complainant is the victim of prejudice or injustice at the hands of the other party."

He huffed and puffed a bit and then endorsed my log book – 'An above average M.E.[22] pilot'.

My year first as a pupil and then as an instructor in Flying Training Command proved to be invaluable. It reinforced, by constant practice (much of it by demonstration to pupil pilots) the automatic reaction to untoward incident in the air. I am convinced that that degree of repetition and automatic and careful adherence to basic principles saved my life when I eventually went on to operational flying. Just as the lack of it sealed the fate of many a young pilot less fortunate in the length and depth of experience. The day came when my repeated requests for posting on to heavy bomber training were answered and I was sent to a Heavy Conversion Unit, first of all to be trained on the Wellington bomber.

---

[22] Multi-engined

7

In the unlikely event that at some time in the future I should find myself being interrogated by St Peter, he might well ask me what, outside inter-personal relationships, had given me most satisfaction and pleasure. Without doubt I would answer, "Flying Lancaster bombers". If he went on to ask of what I was most proud, I would have no hesitation in replying, "Commanding a squadron of Lancasters".

It would, however, be preposterous to imagine that one could go direct from instructing on the obsolescent but wonderful lightweight fighter-bomber the Blenheim 1 to mastering and then commanding a squadron of the even more wonderful super bombing aircraft of World War II, the four engined Lancaster. First one had to acquire a crew: bomb-aimer, navigator, flight engineer, wireless operator and two gunners, mid-upper and rear.

After completing the basic skills in our separate trades and learning the instructions necessary to develop and practice these skills up to operational standards, we were all ushered into a large hanger and instructed to form ourselves into crews. At first meeting it would be crews of five.[23] Crew selection was like an out of control cattle market. The only people who knew one another were those who had trained together in a specific aircrew trade. Axiomatically they could not stay together, not even two best friends, as except for the gunners – who were not recruited into crews until later – there was only one of each speciality in each crew. Unless a pilot noticed a crew member whom he had met before or who, for some almost occult reason, attracted his interest, for the most part the initiative came from the other trades. Amongst the pilots there was one Squadron Leader – a bad choice: he was shot down and made a P.O.W.[24] on his first mission; four or five

---

[23] The two gunners would be added later.

[24] Prisoner of War

Flight Lieutenants, of whom I was one, and then a rather larger number of Flying Officers and Pilot Officers. Rank implied flying experience, so the Squadron Leader and Flight Lieutenants attracted most interest from the sheep who were seeking a bell-wether.

A smart Sergeant wearing Navigator's wings approached me. "Do you want a good navigator, Sir?" he asked. He had with him a report from his navigator training course. There were no obvious black, or even grey, marks. He looked alert. He came from Romford, next outer suburb of London from Ilford, where I had been brought up.

"I'll take a chance", I grinned. "Stay with me whilst we survey the other trades. What's your name?"

"Jimmy", he said. "As a matter of fact", he continued, "I know a good wireless operator. Shall I bring him over?"

"Please do. This process will last for ever if we wait for inspiration".

So he went off and came back with a round-faced, pink cheeked lad wearing wireless operator wings.

"Tell me your name and what you did before you joined the R.A.F."

"I'm Basil. I came from Rugby where I was a milk roundsman".

I could well imagine him treating his customers with boundless good humour. His documents were also in order. So he was enrolled. Next I was approached by the only person I could see amongst the aspirants wearing an officer's uniform. He was a bomb-aimer who had failed his basic pilot training and settled for the next most belligerent role in a bomber aircraft: the man who sighted, aimed and released the bomb. He was a bit older than the others. His name was Scotty. Although quite small, about five foot four at a guess, he was very athletic looking. I was not surprised to discover that he was currently squash champion of his county. I took him on.

Finally I had a diffident approach from a Flight Engineer. He had worked on a farm and was persuaded to go for training as a Flight Engineer on the slender basis that he was experienced at servicing tractors. His name was Len.

So I had my crew:

Bomb-aimer	Scotty	Bank clerk
Navigator	Jimmy	Smart-arse
Wireless Operator	Basil	Cheerful milkman
Flight Engineer	Len	Good with tractors

Later on in our training I had to select two gunners. I was approached by a pair who had made friends with one another during their training. The dominant one was a fair, almost white-haired lad, clearly destined to be known by everybody as Blondie. I did not discover until he was fully integrated with the crew that he had lied from the start about his age. His entire family was killed in an air-raid on Portsmouth. He immediately went to the R.A.F. recruiting office and managed to assure them that he was over 18. He joined my crew fully trained a month before his eighteenth birthday. His friend and sparring partner was also blessed with very clearly distinguished hair. It was red – ginger red. So I acquired a magnificent pair of gunners who became well-known for keenness and efficiency throughout 5 Group: Blondie and Ginger.

We were posted, without the gunners who were to join us at a later date, to Bruntisthorpe, where we were introduced to the two-engined Wellington Bomber. It was robust, its airframe based upon the geodetic construction which was one of the many fertile inventions of Barnes Wallace. It had a very long history of operational service, sharing in the early days the bombing burden with the Hampden, a very much more flimsy twin-engined machine. The Hampden carried on for a year or so, but as its losses increased it was not replaced. It disappeared from front line services. The Wellington, however, continued for another two or three years, holding the fort until it was replaced by the four-engined Stirling, and eventually by the Lancaster and the Halifax. Gradually, as new Lancasters appeared in sufficient numbers, the Wellington and the Stirling did service as training aircraft at the Heavy Conversion Units.

We greatly enjoyed our short training spell on the Wimpey, as the Wellington was called after the cartoon character of J. Wellington Wimpey.[25] It was very robust. Its novel construction was designed to

---

[25] *The twin-engine Wellington was the mainstay of Bomber Command until 1942, when the four-engine heavy bombers entered service. The Wellington prototype took to the air for the first time in June 1936 and production models entered service with the Royal Air Force in October 1938. By September 1939 Bomber Command had eight Wellington squadrons, which increased to 21 by the beginning of 1942. It was widely nicknamed the 'Wimpey' after the character in the Popeye cartoon strip, J. Wellington Wimpey. Wellingtons were the first bombers used to attack Germany in September 1939, but like all British bombers of the war they were lightly armed and suffered heavily from attacks by German fighters. In 1940 the Wellington squadrons were switched to night raids. The unique geodetic latticework construction of the Wellington made it particularly robust - able to sustain remarkable amounts of flak*

limit the extent of damage which could spread when caused by anti-aircraft shells making hits at specific points. In the first great one thousand plus bomber raids to the Ruhr in 1943 and 1944 the Wellingtons played an important role flying below the four-engined aircraft: the Stirlings, the Lancasters and the Halifaxes.

One incident on a training trip in a Wimpey will serve to illustrate its outstanding manoeuvrability for such a heavy aircraft. We were on a cross-country training flight. The purpose was to test all the different specialities amongst the crew. The sky was heavily overcast with thick cloud. We had to find our way by dead reckoning navigation, which involved close cooperation between the wireless operator, whose job was to find bearings of identifiable radio beacons, and the navigator. The navigator then transferred the bearing lines to his maps, making allowance for the distance travelled, thus revealing the position reached where the lines crossed. By this means the navigator pinpointed our position above the earth's surface, calculated the wind-speed and direction and gave the pilot a course to steer to reach his objective which, if the aircraft had flown through the worst of the cloud, should turn out to be some such target as a practice bombing range. On this occasion we were coming back from our target area, ploughing along at about 10,000 feet and cruising at about 180 m.p.h.

One must remember that flying in cloud is not unlike driving in thick fog. At ground level, however, a car can vary its speed and slow down, or even come to a halt, whilst checking for landmarks or consulting maps. Sadly, until the modern inventions of the helicopter and aircraft like the Harrier jet, if any aircraft stopped it would fall out of the sky. The factor of lift, which keeps an aircraft flying, is a function of speed, wing area and drag. If an aircraft speed dropped below a critical level, the aircraft would lose lift, and fall. So, in cloud, one had to keep going. We were flying a compass bearing calculated by the navigator on the basis of radio bearings given by the wireless operator. Suddenly a call

---

damage and yet still keep flying. The last Wellingtons were withdrawn from service over Germany and occupied Europe in 1943 but continued to serve in the Mediterranean theatre and over Burma until the end of the war. The Wellington proved a versatile aircraft and was also employed as a maritime patrol aircraft, a minelayer, and a transport. In all, 11,461 Wellingtons were built during the war, making it the most numerous multi-engine aircraft produced by Britain.

Extract from the Australian War Memorial website.

from base warned us of extreme turbulence and advised that we should come down through cloud at a fast rate of descent. When we reached one thousand feet extreme caution must be exercised. At this point we must lose height very much more carefully. The cloud base in some places near our destination aerodrome was down to five hundred feet.

When the navigator signalled that we were on a course that would bring us to our destination I put the nose of the aircraft down and dived very fast straight ahead. At about one thousand feet the cloud began to thin. Suddenly we broke cloud. An extraordinary phenomenon met my startled gaze. The ground appeared in the top of the windscreen. It probably only took a fraction of a second to realise what had happened. I had dived the aircraft beyond the vertical. We were still going down, but no longer fully the right way up.

No training manual had ever taught what to do in these circumstances. I was below a thousand feet and going down quickly. My training on lighter aircraft came to my aid. I did not think what to do. My muscles just did it. I rolled the aircraft completely over in the direction in which it was turning and held the nose up by pushing on the control column, a completely counter-intuitive manoeuvre.[26] Still losing height, the good old Wimpey, with scarcely a groan of protest, rolled on to its back and then continued until it was flying on an even keel at less than two hundred feet from the ground.

The mere act of writing an autobiography inclines one to overstate one's own cleverness. I have never thought about this incident in terms of my skill. I thanked whatever God looks after aviators that my muscles knew what to do before my head had time to work it out. Continuous practice, and instinct informed by discipline and drill, had saved my life once again – a life put in jeopardy by overweening pride.

Next we were introduced to four-engined aircraft by learning to fly the Stirling. The Stirling was a very agreeable plane. It had its drawbacks from an operational point of view. It could not reach either the height or the straight and level air speed attained by both the Halifax and the Lancaster. I did not fly the Halifax, which Lancaster pilots, probably quite erroneously, held to be inferior to their own machines. It flew higher but did not carry such a heavy weight of bombs. So we felt that we were capable of the more important job.

---

[26] If you are the right way up you pull the control column back to climb. If upside down, climbing is achieved by pushing.

Psychologically we were all taught that the aircraft we were to fly on operations was the best available. I can remember many a friendly argument between Halifax and Lancaster pilots. Both groups were right. *Their* aircraft *was* the best for the job, if that is how they rated it.

* * *

Soon after the war when I was in the House of Commons as an M.P. I asked the Secretary of State for Air how many aircrew were trained throughout the war for service in Bomber Command, and how many were killed, badly wounded, or shot down to become prisoners of war. The Secretary of State was extremely reluctant to give this information, which could only be given in a form available to the public. Eventually he agreed that it would be a written question, the answer to which was circulated on the order paper which went only to M.P.s. After all this time I cannot remember the exact figures. Memory says that the number trained was about 160,000 and the number suffering serious casualty 115,000. A prodigious loss rate. Probably higher over the prolonged period of the whole war than any other branch of any of the services except perhaps for submarines.[27]

Depending on the availability of aircraft and trained crews each crew was scheduled to do 30-35 operations before being 'rested' – i.e. put on other flying duties. If one makes allowance for the crew members who were being trained when the war in Europe finished it meant that, looking at the figures purely statistically, any bomber aircrew member who survived his first sixteen trips was living on borrowed time. When I became a squadron commander and had many administrative duties I was expected not to be able to go on more than three or four missions a month. When I was unable to fly because of other duties my crew were stood down or stood in for the odd members of their trade in other crews who were unavailable through illness or for some other reason. Keenest to keep their numbers up were Blondie and Ginger.

"We didn't join up and get trained so that we could sit on our

---

[27]*Bomber Command…suffered the heaviest casualties of any branch of the Armed Forces during the war, some 60% of its 125,000 aircrew becoming casualties, the vast majority being fatal. 55,500 aircrew were killed, as were 1,570 ground-crew, including 91 members of the Women's Auxiliary Air Force. Extract from Ministry of Defence website 2002*

arses because the Skipper is too busy to fly", they'd say. So they went round the crew room before an operational briefing looking deeply into the faces of other pairs of gunners. "My God!" they'd say. "You do look ill. Run along and see the M.O.[28] We'll fly with your Skipper tonight". The offer was often accepted. When they had each carried out fifty operations I felt they were trying their luck beyond what was reasonable. So I had them each awarded a D.F.M.[29] and posted to instructor duties. They both survived the war.

* * *

We learned to fly as a crew on night operations by doing it. The most dangerous time to fly an aircraft with which one is not familiar is during the first few flights. It is not without significance that the casualty rate was highest amongst crews on their first ten trips. Each of the pilots was sent as an observer/passenger in the aircraft of an experienced pilot to learn whatever his tutor pilot chose to tell him but, in particular, to see for himself what enemy 'flak'[30] looked, smelt and sounded like. If you could hear it or smell it, it was too darned close!

Although I was rated an Above Average Multi-Engined Pilot when I was posted with my crew to 49 Squadron, I was in no way exempt from the norm. In my first ten trips I was twice hit by enemy fire. On one occasion the port outer and starboard inner engines caught fire. Len, my Flight Engineer, was quickly on the ball. He switched off the fuel to the engines on fire. I pressed the appropriate buttons to 'feather' the airscrews.

(The airscrew, our name for the propeller, is driven round and round at speed, scooping back the air, thus driving the whole edifice forward. The blades of the airscrew can be turned so that air pressure is equal on both the front and the back of each blade. The propeller will then stop. Fuel was pumped by the propeller. By stopping its rotation one stops the petrol being pumped.)

Our starboard inner airscrew 'feathered' – stopped turning completely. We could see it still and rigid, doing no good but doing no harm. The port outer, however, had not completely stopped. The

---

[28] Medical Officer

[29] Distinguished Flying Medal

[30] Enemy anti-aircraft shells bursting in the air

feathering motor must have been hit. Consequently the pressure of the wind flowing over the airscrew surfaces caused the blades to 'windmill' – to turn slowly but remorselessly round and round. It was the turning airscrew which operated the pump which sent the fuel into the engine. Every time the propeller completed a circuit it caused a hefty jet of petrol to squirt on to the white hot exhaust pipe, thereby sustaining the fire in that engine, even though the engine itself was switched off. There was only one way left to put out the fire. Blow it out. I put the aircraft into a steep dive. When I thought we were going fast enough I pulled back on the control column as hard as I could. The aircraft effectively stopped before starting to climb. The leaked fuel and flames went on ahead. The fire in the aircraft was out.

The second instance occurred when we were returning from a daylight attack on a flying bomb[31] depot in Northern France. We had hit our target but were fiercely engaged by enemy fighter aircraft. Two engines were incapacitated including the one which activated the compass. We had therefore a badly limping aircraft, and could only steer by judging our position from the position of the sun. We expected to be attacked again by the enemy fighters that had so severely damaged us, but hoped that if we could attract their attention friendly Spitfires would come to our aid. So the bomb-aimer began to broadcast a more or less continuous S.O.S., the international signal of distress for aircraft and shipping. A voice came through on a different channel ordering me to stop the S.O.S. messages. We were in sight of a Lancaster which would come and lead us to safety in England. Eventually a Lancaster appeared and, adjusting its speed to ours, led us westward, across the French coast and over the English Channel.

By this time we had lost height and we could see a Spitfire obviously down at our level to escort us in. Then we saw a Walrus, an amphibious aircraft, one that could land on the sea to pick us up if we had to 'ditch'.[32] Finally we saw an Air Sea Rescue launch coming towards us to provide, if necessary, the same service. None of them were called in to help. We were led towards Ford airport, the aerodrome of Portsmouth. Green flares were sent up giving us permission to come

---

[31] V1

[32] To attempt to land a land-based aircraft on water in the hope that it would float long enough for evacuation

straight in. The flaps would not go down. Clearly the hydraulic system which operated flaps and wheels had been hit. We crossed the airfield boundary very low. The control tower warned us that we had not got our wheels down. High on adrenaline because we were over dry land I called back, "I know. Watch this!" As I reached the airfield proper I punched down the emergency compressed air supply which would send down the wheels. They went down in about ten seconds. Len, the engineer, was looking out of the far-side window. "We've got a puncture in the tyre this side", he shouted.

It was a beautiful sunny afternoon. In front of the control tower people were sitting on the grass. A few of them were enjoying the luxury of deckchairs. They were away to our right, but the puncture was to that side. When the aircraft slowed down and lost lift it would veer to the right. This began to happen. The watchers scattered. The aircraft began to turn in that direction. Before reaching the spectators the right wing tip hit the ground. We spun round and came to a stop.

The aircraft was placed in category AC – complete write-off.[33] The accompanying Lancaster which had come to make sure that we were down safely flew low over us in salute and sped off, presumably to its own home station. We never did discover who the skilful and gallant rescuer was. He will never see this, but it would be cavalier not to acknowledge our deepest gratitude for his courage and skill.[34]

* * *

It would be wrong to imagine that all aircrew under training were saintly fellows who lived no life outside their professional training. Two stories will illustrate what I have in mind.

The wireless operator and the navigator worked closely together. Throughout the squadron whenever their aircraft was airborne the wireless operators took bearings which they passed to their navigator for processing. A record of these trial readings was kept and the appropriate head of each trade kept a record of the skill and vigilance of his men

---

[33] *12,330 Bomber Command aircraft were shot down, wrecked in crashes in the UK or written off due to damage during WW2. Extract from Norfolk and Suffolk Aviation Museum website*

[34] *I asked Ernest if this was the episode for which he received his D.F.C. He wrote back, "No. It came in the post on completion of tour". CM*

throughout the squadron. My two, Jimmy and Basil, regularly featured high up on both lists. So much so that the navigation leader became suspicious. We took Jimmy's logs into the Navigation briefing room and found, to our amazement, that Basil must have been writing down bearings without any attempt at accuracy and Jimmy had been putting them into his logs without plotting them on maps. So the two leaders and I took their log books for the previous month or so and plotted them. We found that we had been in the Indian Ocean and even further afield. On one occasion we were only a mile or so from the South Pole. Or so their records said.

The two delinquents, who had enjoyed lording it for weeks over their fellow tradesmen, were asked to explain. All they could say was that they enjoyed coming out regularly at the top of the competition in their sections. They were forcibly informed that in future all their work would be checked and plotted. Any further dereliction would result in their being stripped of their trade badges and reduced to the lowest rank of airman, AC2,[35] and a life for the rest of their service of the lowest of menial tasks. Each of them carried on with their careers but with very different outcomes. With Basil it consisted of a brush with the civilian police.

One day he was marched in before me accompanied by a civilian police sergeant. He had been caught in a railway wagon in a top secret siding beside the local station with a young woman. In flagrante delicto. The policeman wanted to know how I would react to my sergeant (he was in fact in my crew) being hauled up before the local magistrate on charges of trespass and even of espionage. I managed to convince him that he could safely hand him over to the R.A.F. and we would deal with it. There was at that time a unit at Sheffield run by the R.A.F. military police, known as the Aircrew Disciplinary Refresher School. It was established to deal with offences which the service did not consider important enough to take valuable and expensively trained members of aircrew out of action for an indefinite time. Some civilian magistrates had been giving custodial sentences to military personnel who had come up before them.

I duly delivered my lecture on the iniquity of being caught, and sentenced Basil to two weeks at the Disciplinary Refresher School, where I knew from reports that the regime was fierce and the physical exercises

---

[35] Aircraftsman Class 2

strenuous. Basil left to make his way to Sheffield. The next morning, to my amazement, he reappeared in front of me. He had been sent back. Upon his arrival he had had a medical. The doctor had diagnosed flat feet. He could not, on medical grounds, undergo the course. He had gone into the Sergeants' Mess where a lively game of poker was about to start. He was invited to join in. When he got up at the end of the game he had won some £27, a lot of money for a lad whose pay could not have been more than £2 a day. I did not obey my instinct, which was to burst out laughing, and he left my presence swearing to be better behaved in future. Jimmy had a different and sadder fate.

We were caught in heavy searchlights over Darmstadt one night. Flak was bursting all round. We could see it, hear it beating our airframe and, most frightening of all, we could smell it. The only thing to do in the circumstances is to hurl one's aircraft about the sky, constantly changing height and direction but maintaining a general course towards a clear sky, preferably in the direction of home. In that way one hoped that the operators of the anti-aircraft guns would not be able to guess where you would be when the shells reached their predicted direction and height. In the midst of this frenzy of violence, with the inside of the aircraft from time to time lit up by such a concentration of searchlights that one could have read a newspaper, I became aware of Jimmy, the navigator, leaning over me and, putting all his maps and charts on my lap, saying, "I can't cope any more".

We had dropped our bomb load and were on our way back home. Without relaxing my violent handling of the aircraft I called Scotty, the bomb-aimer, who was the other member of the crew who had some training in navigation. He took over the maps and the other papers.

"I will fly as accurately as I can due west (270 degrees) for ten minutes. We have, I think, just bombed Darmstadt. Lay off ten minutes on 270 degrees and then work out a course to steer direct to the U.K."

I told Jimmy to keep out of everybody's way. Miraculously we got home safely, largely thanks to the skill of Scotty, our reserve navigator. When we landed back at base and were debriefed I made a short statement about what Jimmy had done. Nobody perhaps has a stronger recognition of the importance of total cooperation and trust which all crew members must have with one another when flying, especially when heavily engaged by night defences over enemy territory. But we got out of it, and all came home. One of our number had cracked. The strain had been too much. Had I known what would happen to him, I would not have reported the incident. I would have recommended him for extended leave to see whether he could recover his nerve. Instead of, as I had expected, a medical investigation of his behaviour and condition he had to face disciplinary procedures. Unlike the Army the R.A.F. never use the expression 'cowardice in the face of the enemy'; they use the awful refined expression, 'lack of moral fibre'.

Faced with the – to him – certainty of imminent death Jimmy had lost the will and ability to continue to function. He was stripped of his navigator's badge and reduced to the lowest airman rank. I came across him a year or so later, shuffling around, wearing a dirty uniform, plimsolls on his feet, cleaning toilets. I called to him, but he would not look at me. I have rarely felt more sympathy with someone's plight, nor anger with myself at not having foreseen what would happen when I reported the incident. Also, I could not help wondering if those who condemned him to such a dreadful fate had themselves ever been faced with circumstances too dreadful to bear.

8

Management teaching, whether for industry, commerce or the services, usually emphasises that without good leadership it is unreasonable to expect enthusiastic and efficient work lower down in the pecking order. One rarely has the opportunity to experience outstanding examples of the two types of leader in immediate succession, and to observe the effect of each on those under their command. When I was posted to a squadron to begin my operational career in Lancasters I was very fortunate, since I was going to experience the two types of leader, to work under them in the order of the 'good' leader first.

We were posted to 49 Squadron. It had as good a record as any squadron in Bomber Command: two Victoria Crosses, several D.S.O.s[36].and an above average number of D.F.C.s[37], an award often presented to pilots who had successfully completed a tour of thirty to thirty five sorties. The average number of sorties completed by pilots of Bomber Command was sixteen or seventeen. 49 Squadron therefore had a record which was about twice as good as the Command average. This was in spite of the fact that for the first year or so of the war they were flying in the more fragile Hampden.

The C.O. of 49 when I joined was an ebullient extrovert. He had the habit of 'buzzing' the home aerodrome at every opportunity, especially upon his return from a successful operation. Buzzing is to fly very, very low at maximum speed over the ground, buildings and runways of aerodromes or even church spires. Because of this exuberant habit he was know throughout the command as 'Buzz' Botting. Higher authority looked askance at the example he gave to his crews. He preached a different gospel, however. "Don't do as I do, do as I say". And what he said was, in effect: "I am just showing off. It is a great release of tension – *for me*. But it is very, very dangerous. I would be a

---

[36] Distinguished Service Order
[37] Distinguished Flying Cross

hypocrite to give an order forbidding you to do what I do. However, I strongly advise you not to." Both the aircrews and the ground staff loved him for his example of joie de vivre, carried out with the highest flying skills.

I came to 49 Squadron to start my operational flying career. I was already an Above Average pilot and quickly mastered the moods, such as they were, of the Lancaster. In the last chapter I detailed two sorties which nearly went badly wrong. I was fulfilling the statistical expectation of having one's shakiest trips amongst one's first ten sorties. I was immensely fortunate that we had a Squadron Commander who was ready to talk seriously but cheerfully about near-calamities. But he also emphasised again and again that the most dangerous flying situations have a chance of being survived if one exercised – boldly and without hesitation – the mastery over the machine that can only be achieved by active and deliberate experimentation. There were pilots who had never flown a Lancaster with one engine cut. Buzz flew with all his pilots at least once and sometimes more. No 49 Squadron crew was released for operations by the C.O. until he had flown with them and, as a practice emergency, he had switched off not one but two engines. Wing Commander Buzz Botting was a great leader. We all loved him: me not less than anyone else. 49 was a marvellous and successful squadron into which to be posted. Under Botting's leadership the successes of the Squadron's historic career was fully maintained.

44 Squadron was in many ways the complete antithesis of 49. It was the only Rhodesian Squadron, certainly in 5 Group, and probably in Bomber Command. We were never told of the precise financial and/or political reasons for the existence of a Rhodesian bomber squadron. There were one or two consequences of this provenance. First, the C.O. had to be a Rhodesian, if there was one available in Bomber Command of sufficient experience and seniority. Second, the Squadron was provided with an apparently inexhaustible supply of Rhodesian tobacco and cigarettes. They were of a type called 'From C to C'. The small print indicated that this meant 'From Cape to Cairo', but such was the quality of the tobacco that only extreme poverty towards the end of the month encouraged members of the Squadron to avail themselves of the plentiful free supply of 'C to C' cigarettes. These were known as 'From Camel to Consumer'. One could tell that the end of the month was approaching and that funds were getting low as first a trickle and then a flood of sergeants and officers could be seen – and smelt – smoking this nauseous emblem of Imperial solidarity.

This, however, is about the Squadron Commander. When I was posted to 44 Squadron, Wing Commander Thompson had completed his tour of operations and was waiting to be posted away. He did not vacate the C.O.'s office or accommodation, although he was no longer in command. Behind his desk, attached to the wall, was coiled a long, fierce-looking ox-hide whip. Whenever he had an airman in on a disciplinary charge or, worse, a charge of performing a duty less than perfectly, Wing Commander Thompson – known as 'Bull' Thompson – would, before giving the maximum sentence for the offence permitted by the King's Regulations, look around at the whip on the wall and then back at the offending airman, saying, "I wish I was back in Rhodesia". Not surprisingly, Bull Thompson was feared, but neither liked nor respected.

When I arrived on posting from 49 to 44 Squadron morale was low. It was impolitic to release figures showing losses squadron by squadron, but the report of each raid gave the losses. It seemed to us, who were posted in from other squadrons to bolster morale in the crew room, that the losses from 44 Squadron featured with greater frequency than those of other squadrons. My crew was one of those transferred to boost morale and performance. I happened to be the senior in rank, a Flight Lieutenant of at least a year's seniority. A Bomber Command Squadron normally comprised two Flights. Each Flight had a Squadron Leader commander under the overall command of the C.O. of the Squadron, who held the rank of Wing Commander. Within a night or so of our arrival, both Squadron Leaders were missing on the same operation. Wing Commander Thompson, although now no longer Squadron Commander, was still on the station awaiting posting. It is quite likely he was waiting to be posted back to Rhodesia. His posting would certainly have had a political element. I was therefore left as the senior officer, although only a Flight Lieutenant, of a squadron in which morale was low, losses had been above average, the much disliked former C.O. was still on the premises and a search was in hand for political reasons to find a Rhodesian officer of sufficient experience to take over this very difficult appointment. Although I was fortunate in being permitted to bring two experienced crews of my own choice from 49 Squadron, I must say the prospect filled me with dismay.

There then occurred the extraordinary incident of the 5 Group Conference of Senior Officers. This meeting of squadron commanders and above was to determine the rest of my career in Lancasters.[38] I was the only officer below the rank of Wing Commander at the conference. It was in the nature of things that I was the only one present currently flying on operations more than once or twice a month. The other officers present all had heavy training and administrative duties. I cannot begin to guess what sort of job I would have made if I had been left, especially as a comparatively junior officer, in command of a squadron at such a low ebb as 44 Squadron. Fortunately my experience at speaking my mind in a clear, outright fashion carried me through. The fact that I was the only pilot present currently carrying out a full range of operational duties gave some credence to my dissenting voice. I think I had also made the point that I had spent over a year as an instructor on multi-engined aircraft and was talking from a wealth of experience not currently shared by the other participants. This added to my credibility. Finally I was angry that men with no recent experience of the world of operational flying were laying down the law about the risks 'we' were prepared to take, but which would have to be taken by raw and inexperienced crews. I also knew that as the most junior pilot in the room I had no temporary rank or status that could be taken from me. So I spoke up.

R.A.F. Balderton

---

[38] *See Preface for the full story*

Within a month I was a Wing Commander, promoted to form my own squadron. I was allowed, an extraordinary concession, to choose four crews from 44 Squadron to form the nucleus of 227, as my new squadron was to be called. I still hear once or twice a year from Gordon McLusker who writes from a retirement home in Australia, and from Mervyn Croker, from a similar establishment in New Zealand. Their message, repeated year by year – and both saying the same thing – is of thanks that I chose them to join me in my new squadron. They are not so grateful as I am at having made such wise choices.

The war was moving towards an end. German defences were getting very weak. We had been sent upon a series of arduous and highly dangerous missions. We attacked the enemy's supply of oil day and night: in Eastern Germany, Romania and Czechoslovakia. I can still see as I write, even without closing my eyes, columns of flame reaching sometimes as high as eight or nine thousand feet as the bombing successfully eliminated oil installations upon which the last hours of the Third Reich depended.[39]

There was a touch of cynical nastiness which must have had a devastating effect on German morale. High over our heads flew an aircraft wired up with the most modern of radio transmitting equipment. Each aircraft had its contingent of listeners and writers and of fluent German speakers. As bombs rained down on the Reich a running commentary was sent out, via German radio stations (for the boffins had found a way to cut out German transmissions from their own stations and to replace them with Allied propaganda). The culmination of each programme was always the same. An unedited edition of a Hermann Goering broadcast to the German people in 1940 in which he promised, "Not an enemy bomb will fall on the sacred land of Germany". I still feel a little bit ashamed. Perhaps it was no worse than what I was doing.

It would be misleading to give the impression that these prodigiously long journeys, with combat over defended targets at the end, were without serious casualty. Part of the morale-set of my crews was –

---

[39] When the Armistice was declared, some of us were taken in turns to see what we had achieved. It was not the devastated towns, terrible though the sight was, that most impressed me. It was the sight of rows of magnificent fighter aircraft concreted into fixed positions in the ground, not being used to prevent our bombers attacking Berlin and the other great centres of population, industry and administration, but being used as anti-tank guns because they had no fuel with which to fly.

1. That they knew that every day another great stretch of Western and Central Europe was passing into the hands of Allied soldiers. For the first time in the War to bale out of a badly-damaged aircraft meant a more than average change of falling (literally) into friendly hands;
2. The battle for fuel was being won, and with it effective opposition lessened; and
3. The crews of 227 were convinced (and I did nothing to disabuse them) that even on these terribly long flights to Eastern Europe *our* losses were considerably less than those of other squadrons.

In fact by that stage in the War details of losses were no longer publicised. High morale, because we knew that a victorious outcome was inevitable and close at hand, needed no lying boosts.

I do remember an emergency call that we had over the Christmas period of 1944. The Germans had concentrated the maximum force of heavy armour, tanks and mobile artillery, that they could muster. They brought them surreptitiously to the Eastern side of the forest of Ardennes. On Christmas Day they started a major attack. It made a remarkable advance. Opposite them were at least an equal number of American tanks. I would not like to be accused of anti-American prejudice. There may also have been other vehicles of war belonging to Britain and other allies. It is said that all the senior officers of the Allied armies were whooping it up in Brussels. There was nobody to give command orders to man the vehicles and to counter attack. The R.A.F. was called in. Fortunately intelligence was good and we were soon informed accurately where the enemy concentrations were at their most thick. I can remember two little towns, Houfallize and St Vith, which were controlling the break out. We repeatedly bombed, at low level, their concentrations of armour. I do not think for one moment that an overwhelming victory would have changed the course of the war for the Germans. However, the fact that the Air Force broke up the attack and brought a halt to a gallant but fruitless attempt to stay the Allied advance prevented a major morale boost to the enemy and enabled some of the Allied army Brass Hats to hide their shame at a major display of self-indulgence.

* * *

The reader may find a few technical paragraphs of interest and a help in understanding what we had to do. First, let me describe a most successful device worked out by our boffins which we called Window. Strips of aluminium foil of a scientifically determined width and length were released in bundles from very high flying aircraft. As they spread out they gave the same return to enemy radar as would a large flight of aircraft. If it was required to create a diversion a small number of aircraft would set off in a misleading direction, giving the impression of a considerable sized raid. A little later the main attack would set off in an entirely different direction vastly aided by the fact that the enemy defences had been alerted in the wrong place by a small specialist force. Many main force bombing attacks were made less arduous and losses considerably diminished because defences were foiled by this simple, effective but comparatively inexpensive device. This is only one small debt we owed to the constant research and invention of the technical branch of the service.

It may also be of interest and value to go over the steps taken in planning an operation. Targets were grouped under a number of headings: Army Support, Economic, Attacks on Civilian Morale, Aid to Naval Operations – and so on. Of the incidents which I have already described, clearly the intervention in the Ardennes at Christmas was an essential piece of Army support; the sustained war on natural and synthetic oil production was aimed at an invaluable group of economic targets; the devastation of cities like Brunswick, Hamburg and Dresden, together with sustained attacks on Berlin, must have diverted a considerable proportion of German military to the defence of the centres of civilian population; whilst constant attacks all along the Channel and Atlantic seaboards on U-boat pens were designed to reverse what had been for years the domination by the Germans of the Atlantic.

The decision as to the type of attack immediately called for was made at the highest level. One knows from other histories that the Prime Minister took a personal interest and was from time to time very forceful about what the war situation called for.

The political decision, advised by the Imperial General Staff, was conveyed to Air Chief Marshal Sir Arthur Harris who had the unenviable task of deciding what resources had to be put towards carrying out the decision. The A.C.M.[40] has had a very bad press, especially from the traditionally more liberal papers. After the War he wrote a book called

---

[40] Air Chief Marshal

The Bomber Offensive. It was reviewed in the New Statesman by Michael Foot under the heading, 'The Offensive Bomber'. I treasure the fact that when the New Statesman published a long piece from me defending the unfortunate senior officer who daily had the terrible task of sending young men off to certain death and of causing devastation to life and property on the ground, I received a letter from two children, aged eight and ten, who lived next door to Sir Arthur. They thanked me for coming to 'Uncle Arthur's' defence, and assured me that the elderly gentleman who came in from time to time and played parlour games on the floor with them could not be the monster some people thought him.

On receipt of the political decision naming the type of target, and frequently the specific target that had been selected, Harris would consult with his staff: meteorologists to forecast the weather on the night selected for the raid; the Air staff who would have a complete schedule, by squadron number and type of aircraft, of the aircraft that would be available; the armourers with an accurate statement of the nature, size and number of the bombs available for the proposed mission, and many others of less obvious but equally vital importance.

A specific potential target having been selected, specialist navigators would then sketch in on a master map of Europe alternative routes to and from the target, consulting Intelligence specialists who would have the latest information, drawn from reconnaissance air photography and any other reliable sources of information. Each route would be measured. The mileage, with an extra safety margin, would be translated into gallons of fuel, and the gallons converted into weight. This would leave a weight which could be converted into the appropriate amount available for the bomb load. The equation was precise:

$$AUW = WoA + WoF + WoB^{41}$$

Bombs varied from 100 lb and 200 lb High Explosives; 400 lb, packed with incendiaries; 400 lb High Explosive; 1000 lb and 2000 lb High Explosives. Towards the end of the War aircraft were modified to be able to take very large bombs of 10,000 lb and even 20,000 lb High Explosive.

---

[41] AUW is All Up Weight at takeoff
WoA is Weight of Aircraft, equipment and crew
WoF is Weight of Fuel
WoB is Weight of Bomb load available to destroy target.

The decision would then be made as to the weight and therefore the quantity of fuel, and the precise type of bombs and the number of each. The weight of the bomb-load could then be calculated. The number and type of aircraft needed to convey the bomb load would be worked out. Thus it could be calculated precisely what bombs, adding up to what weight, could be carried, using how much fuel. Clearly a very long journey would result in a reduced bomb load, and vice versa.

Bomber Command Headquarters would then decide from the availability lists, submitted by the Group Headquarters daily, who would be charged with the responsibility for the raid. Each Group Commander whose group was detailed to be involved would summon a conference by scrambler telephone[42] of Base Commanders (units of three squadrons) and Squadron Commanders. Each would have their appropriate specialist officers listening in. By this means the decision of the Commander-in-Chief would be translated through Group Commanders to Squadron Commanders with precise orders about the name of the target (usually in code in case the chain of information was somehow penetrated), the route, the types of aircraft to be used, the fuel load and the bomb load of each aircraft.

At an appropriate number of hours before the scheduled time of takeoff, specialist leaders – navigation leader, signals leader, bombing leader – would have in all the crew members of their trade and give them a technical briefing, usually without yet naming the target. All the crews would then come together, equipped with flying clothes, maps and charts, and signal papers. They would be taken into a large briefing room and the doors locked, with a guard armed against unauthorised observers – neither spies nor nosey-parkers could be party to the definitive information of a raid. The party of senior officers would then come in. The Station and Base Commanders would usually be present, but the responsibility for the briefing rested with the Squadron Commander. He would unveil the target on a large wall map. Either the Squadron Commander and the Station Intelligence Officer, or both, would give a briefing on the importance of the target.

Although the navigators had been separately briefed, the route would be gone over. Briefing would be given by the I.O.[43] of any last

---

[42] A system whereby the signals of the sender were broken up and could only be unscrambled by recipients with appropriate receivers

[43] Intelligence Officer

minute information such as movement of enemy defences or any other relevancies that had just come in. The final words of warning and advice came from the Squadron Commander who, in any case, would as likely as not be flying with them. Sometimes the Base Commander felt that he too had to say a word. The briefing conference then broke up and the crews departed to find their aircraft, make their checks and await the signal to start engines, taxi out and take off.

Although in theory crews went straight to their aircraft, some of them had little rituals which released their tensions but did not take up much time. One of them, Flying Officer Richardson, was a professional pianist. As soon as the briefing was over he went to a piano. If he was excited by the challenge of the target he would hammer out something magnificent, probably by Wagner. If his reaction was neutral he would play something more gentle and less classical; the theme from a current musical, for example. If he was disturbed by the news he would play a few quiet bars of blues music. I am sure it did him good. He survived the war. His crew always stayed to listen to him. Not, I think, influenced by his choice of mood but as a gesture of respect and solidarity.

Reporting on these things after an interregnum of sixty years I am flattered to realise how central to the whole process was the Squadron Commander. I ask myself, "Was that really me?" and am forced to an amazed confession – "Yes! It really was!"

* * *

But above all I am constantly amazed at the enormous intellectual, psychological and spiritual burden placed upon one man, Air Chief Marshal Harris, the Commander-in-Chief of Bomber Command. Every day information from many sources had to be taken on board and absorbed. The technical problems of weather, availability of appropriate aircraft and crews, the availability of the appropriate bombs and ammunition for the machine guns with which his crews would attempt to defend themselves, the direction of sortie and, above all, the terrible price in young lives of each of his decisions. Even if he concealed the agony daily brought about by the need for decisions, which was his and his alone, we now know the terrible strain under which he lived for nearly six years.

To add to his burden, gradually the 'liberal' press increased its critical pressure. To us he was 'Bert'; officially he was 'Sir Arthur', but to news media like the New Statesman and the News Chronicle he was known as 'Butch' Harris, or even as 'The Butcher'. It is, in my view, a national disgrace that whereas the other Commanders-in-Chief, in the R.A.F. as well as other services, received honours and awards when the war was over, Air Chief Marshal Sir Arthur Harris retired to his native South Africa unhonoured by an Establishment which seemed to be completely in accord with the 'liberal' critics.

I confronted Michael Foot some years later. I asked him if he knew about German concentration camps, the determination of Hitler and the Nazis to eliminate the Jewish population of Europe by the most hideous of means, the expressed ambition of the German political leaders to conquer the world and to submit its peoples to the continuous reign of terror. I cannot remember a single suggestion from him other than that we should negotiate a peaceful settlement of problems by example and by diplomacy. He found no answer when I asked him to imagine being surrounded by an angry group of hungry, man-eating tigers. Would he refuse guns and whips and seek to negotiate a peaceful settlement? Again, no answer.

The justification of the terrible loss of life and property, both of our own allies and of the enemy, was that there seemed then and seems now to be no alternative to fighting, if necessary to the end. I make no apologies for having played my part.

* * *

There are in all walks of life two main styles of leadership. There is the leader who can perform in an outstandingly successful way himself each of the tasks which his subordinates are called upon to perform, and the leader who can set out in detail what he wants each of his subordinates to do and then uses the force of rank or personality to see that his wishes are carried out. The military services provide many examples of the two types of leader.

The contrast is, in my experience, best exemplified by two Air Officers commanding groups in the RAF: Air Vice Marshall Don Bennett, who commanded 8 Group, and Air Vice Marshall Ralph Cochrane, commander of 5 Group. They had both reached that eminence sharing many of the same technical qualities. If Bennett were perhaps the better navigator, then Cochrane was the better pilot.

Because of his navigation skills, Bennett was a natural to form and command the Pathfinder group. Their job was to find and mark targets for the main bombing squadrons to release their bombs on.

Cochrane set out to be the best pilot, the best bomb aimer and the best navigator in 5 Group. It is said that whenever the A.O.C. went onto the practice range as a pilot, for example, he took the best available navigator and bomb aimer in his team. He was then able to show in all three skills the best results in his group.

It is said that bribes were offered to the other two members of his team to perform less than their best on any training run. The rumour is probably apocryphal. If true, there is no doubt that nobody would have dared spoiled the A.O.C.'s training run. In the event, Bennett laid down standards, particularly of navigation, for his crews. Cochrane was able to say: "I can do it, and I am human. So can you if you work at it." Gradually 5 Group pilots, bomb aimers and navigators under Cochrane's leadership set up their own pathfinding squadron and were thus able to operate independently of 8 Group.

9

You will have gathered by now that I had been fortunate enough to have gained the experience and to have been awarded the grading of Above Average (*not* Superior) as a Multi-Engined Pilot, and also an Above Average Instructor. Perhaps it would be appropriate to put the two qualifications together and to take you on an operational flight over enemy territory one night in, say, October 1944. Not yet mid-winter, but quite dark fairly early.

We go out to our Lancaster. You are a newly qualified Lancaster operational pilot who has not yet flown in anger. You are about to get a Cook's Tour running commentary on what we see and hear. At the aircraft we go through a series of checks which range from ensuring the engines are in good working order and that the bomb doors are closed and locked, to simple but important details such as checking that none of the tyres are punctured. Once in the cockpit the checks continue.

(There is a dreadful story of a pilot who took it for granted that all his flying controls were connected properly – so that when he pulled back the control the elevators on the tail would come down causing the aircraft to climb, and when he pressed his right rudder control the rudder would move to the right, causing the aircraft to turn to the right. When he took off, he reached the appropriate speed and pulled back on his control column. Instead of climbing gently off the ground, the nose of the aircraft went down instead of up. He was racing towards a hedge. There was a gap to the right of him. He trod hard on his right rudder and the aircraft started to move to the left. He must have been a very good pilot because he realised at once that his controls were connected to operate in the reverse way to what was expected. He straightened the take-off run by pressing hard on his left rudder. The aircraft moved to the right. He then pressed the control column forward and the aircraft took off. With superb skill selecting the opposite use of control column and rudder to what was instinctive he managed to do a tight circuit and land without damaging himself or his aircraft.

Rumour has it that he was awarded an immediate A.F.C[44] for his superb flying, and also received a severe reprimand for not having done his essential checks before starting engines. If he had operated the rudder controls he would have looked out of the window and seen that they were working in reverse. Similarly one of the checks which he failed to carry out was to push his control column forward and look out to see that the elevators moved for descent and vice versa.)

We have gone out to our aircraft and carried out all the checks and found that everything is in order. The sergeant in charge of the ground crew who has prepared the aircraft for flight receives a signature confirming that the machine is in order and has been taken over by the pilot. The rest of the crew, having courteously greeted the passenger, climb into their allotted places: navigator behind the main spar (a thick girder which connects the wings of the fuselage); the wireless operator behind the navigator; mid-upper and rear gunners to their turrets; the bomb-aimer sits on a step down from the main cockpit (rather than in the nose of the aircraft), whilst the flight engineer busies himself checking gauges as the aircraft starts up and taxis out ready for take-off. You, the passenger, are stowed somewhere near the pilot. Special provision for passengers has not been made by the manufacturer. A signal is given from the control tower and the aircraft of the squadron begin to line up fairly close to one another on the perimeter track and to move slowly forward until the leading aircraft is beside the upwind end of the runway to be used for take-off. It turns on to the end of the runway. The control tower signals with a green Aldis lamp and it takes off.

When our turn comes we turn on to the end of the runway and put on our brakes. An aircraft with a full load of petrol and bombs needs maximum possible speed for take-off. Opening the throttles, we bear down hard on the brakes – we hold the aircraft straining to get off until we also receive a green 'all clear for take-off' signal. The brakes come off and with a sigh of relief the Lancaster leaps forward and as I open all four throttles we rapidly gather speed down the runway. I keep the aircraft straight by gentle use of the rudders, and by correcting any tendency to swing by opening the throttles of those engines towards which we might swing to help keep us going straight.

---

[44] A.F.C – Air Force Cross for distinguished flying other than against the enemy.

The propellers of the aircraft may be designed to rotate in a clockwise or anticlockwise direction. The rotation of four engines all turning in an anticlockwise direction, as in a Lancaster, sets up a force known as *torque* which seeks to swing the aircraft, when on the ground rolling for take-off, to the left. A heavily laden aircraft must therefore, as it gathers speed for take-off, be constantly and carefully corrected to prevent it veering off the straight line it needs for a safe and satisfactory 'unsticking'.[45] At the speed laid down for the present all-up weight I slowly pull back on the control column and the aircraft takes to the air. On the ground it has been a large and cumbersome crawler. As soon as it is airborne, our Lancaster is a bird – a great, graceful, beautiful bird.

Once sure that we are safely airborne I select 'Up' on the lever that controls the wheels and, at my command, the flight engineer takes up the flaps a few degrees at a time to prevent too violent a change in lift.

Airborne and trimmed for a steady climb, we go straight ahead to clear the environs of the airfield then turn gently to the left to take our place amongst the other aircraft from our own airfield and the two or three others which are very close, for we are in flat Lincolnshire, site of many war-time airfields and often with aircraft taking off on the same mission from several airfields at the same time. If it is dusk or dark all the aircraft will be showing navigation lights. The risk of collision is very great when as many as forty or fifty machines, heavy with fuel and bombs, take off very close to one another in time and space.

We like to be as close as possible on take off, because later we will be flying near to one another in the dark skies of Europe for our mutual safety. I may be exaggerating, but I seem to remember 227 Squadron getting twelve aircraft airborne in about five minutes. Good discipline, good flying, maximum vigilance and an eye to what will be best for us all. Our target tonight is Brunswick, so we set course at about 065 degrees, north-north-east. We do not want to go due east for this would take us near the heavy defences of the Ruhr. I must explain things to my passenger as the flight goes on.

We have decided to go low over the North Sea, entering Europe between Leewarden and Groningen in Holland, still flying very low down, hoping to go undetected by radar. Half an hour before us two flights would have taken off, also for Germany. The first would consist

---

[45] Unsticking – implies that the aircraft is 'stuck' to the ground until flying speed is reached

of five Mosquitoes flying very high and dropping quantities of 'window'[46]. They would fly between Hamburg and Bremen, alerting the defences of these two important target towns, but would continue, very high and very fast as though making for Berlin. The other flight, also of Mosquitoes carrying 'window', would divert southwards as though making for the Ruhr.

If you look at the map you will see that to fly between two heavily defended areas, one round Bremen and Hamburg to the north and the other to the south, towards the massive industrial conurbation of the Ruhr, will bring their heaviest anti-aircraft gun and fighter aircraft defences into action. As you can see there are considerable signs of enemy activity on both sides: flashes of guns on the ground; clouds of smoke as flak shells burst in the sky, and searchlights seeking – as their name implies – to illuminate any aircraft which appear to be flying in their neighbourhood. With luck, and we seem to having a lot of luck this evening, we are having a fairly clear passage in the corridor between the two heavily defended areas. You may have seen an aircraft with half a dozen searchlight beams focused upon it. Searchlights are not directly lethal, but they give a strong indication, if not a clear view, of an intruder aircraft. This greatly facilitates night-fighters in their search for the invader and the crews of the anti-aircraft guns who are seeking to shoot it down.

Our bird is a wily bird. He has, as you may be able to discern, varied his speed and altitude and is continuously changing direction. Look: he has eluded the searchlights and stands a good chance of getting back on track for his own target, Brunswick. The skies are clear of hostile defence.

Suddenly – "Corkscrew port!". The shout is from the rear gunner. He must have glimpsed a night fighter. I hurl the aircraft into a steep diving turn to the left. At the bottom of my dive I call, "Changing course. Climbing starboard". If the night fighter had in fact been following us the gunners had a short-lived steady platform at the bottom of the dive to attack it. We seem to have evaded him. I get back on a course which will take us north of Hamburg. Again, as you can see, there are strong indications of defence activity as we pass a few miles north of Hamburg. We turn and fly south-by-south-west towards Brunswick.

Look straight ahead. Now a little to the right. Can you see a glow

---

[46] See Chapter 8 for description and function of window

in the sky? Good. That means that the Pathfinder boys are already engaged in 'marking' the target. As we get nearer you will see the bright lights in the sky. They are called 'chandelier' flares. They are dropped over the target from high above, and when they light up the light is intense enough, even on the darkest night – indeed, especially on the darkest night – to enable one to read a newspaper in the streets below. By the light of the flares the Controller of the operation, who tonight is flying in a Mosquito, is looking for the agreed aiming point. Tonight it is a bend in the river. (In Munich, it is a kidney-shaped sports field a little outside the town on the south west side.) When he has identified the aiming point he will either drop a coloured marker on it himself, or he will call in one of his support crews to mark it. Tonight it will be a red marker.

There it goes. We can see it burning on the ground ahead of us. Then a yellow marker right on top of the red. The Controller is not satisfied with the accuracy of the first red marker and has called for it to be cancelled by having a yellow marker dropped on top of it. These markers are a very special type of firework. It is calculated that each will burn for about half an hour and cannot be put out by normal fire fighting apparatus on the ground. Another red is going down. It has been assessed by the Controller and found good. He orders the other marker aircraft to drop their markers on the second red. As you can see, all this is going on as we move with our bomb-load towards the target. When the markers are all down and we have a good clear patch of red fire at which to aim, we are called in to drop our bombs. We may be told to aim at the nearest edge of the red fires. Or the furthest. Or a bit to the left, or a bit to the right. The Controller is responsible for giving the bombing aircraft information, as accurately as possible, of precisely where to aim.

I live in France nowadays. One day a French neighbour was clearing out his dressing table drawers. One drawer was lined with a copy of the local newspaper – the Sud-Ouest. It contained a vivid account of a raid on the gunpowder factory which is about ten miles from my house. The report gave a description of the raid, starting with the flares. They warned the civilian population to seek shelter. Most ran away on the only road opposite which went for about a mile into the heart of a vineyard. From this vantage point they could see the busy little Mosquitoes laying down their markers. Then the bombers came over. According to this newspaper report every bomb but one fell within the perimeter walls of the powder factory. Of the seven buildings in the enclave, six were hit and completely demolished. The only casualties amongst the civilian population were a fifteen year old boy, who was so fascinated by what he was seeing that he refused to look for shelter, and the victim of the only bomb that failed to hit the target. It fell on open ground near the neighbouring village of Cours de Piles. The shaking of the ground rattled the cottages and afterwards an old peasant was heard to complain that the vibrations had shaken off a shelf his year's supply of goose fat, broken the glass containers and ruined his fat supply. Small price in the conduct of a great war for an attack which robbed the enemy of the output of a gunpowder factory. It was valuable corroboration, forty years on, of the kind of accuracy we managed to achieve.

As we get nearer you can see the flares falling and eventually fading. On the ground there is a red marker cancelled by two yellows. Further red markers accumulate in a patch. The Controller is calling us in: "Aim as near as you can to the centre of the reds". The most frustrating thing for a Controller is the phenomenon known as 'creep back'. Remember that the crews will be with a skipper who may have only been on a few trips. He may only be twenty years old. He is inexperienced, but has got to the target. He instructs his bomb-aimer to drop his bombs as soon as he can see the marker in his bombsight. The bomb-aimer will also be young and inexperienced. He can see that they are tracking so that they will arrive over the target. As soon as he has a clear view of the red markers, but not 'as near as you can get to the centre of the reds', he presses the bomb release button. The bombs fall and explode too soon. The next aircraft may aim at the explosions and a whole chain of bombs may be dropped off the target, prematurely released. Result: partial failure of the raid.

In our own aircraft we are approaching steadily. Our little foray with the night fighter brings us in about 2,000 feet below the briefed height. The bulk of the flak is bursting higher than we are flying. We can see the red marker cancelled by the yellows. Just ahead of them is the big concentration on the ground of reds. We hear the Controller call us in to aim at the 'centre of the reds'. The bomb-aimer takes over directing the flight. "Left, left.....r-i-i-i-i-ght.....steady......left, left a little..." The pilot obeys with slight movements of the controls. From our vantage point we can see the nose of the aircraft getting more accurately aimed.

"Bombs doors open". The bomb doors are opened. A few final corrections, then "Bombs gone!". There is little need to report that the bombs have gone – as they are released the aircraft goes up as though in a lift. The bomb aimer makes an inspection and reports that every bomb has gone. "Bomb doors closed".

Then come the most stressful few seconds of the attack. The release of the bombs activates a camera which exposes a film for the few seconds that it takes for the bombs to reach the ground. The aircraft continues at the same speed, but the bombs drop in a parabolic curve and will hit the ground after the aircraft has passed over the point of impact. To get an accurate picture of the point of impact, badly needed by the Intelligence department which will be assessing the accuracy of the raid, the camera is set with figures of height, direction and wind speed. From the moment of 'Bombs gone' the aircraft must be flown with great accuracy for the number of seconds that it will take for the bombs to reach the ground. If the target is well protected, as in a few minutes we will find Brunswick to be, the thought of flying through predicted flak for even a few seconds is very nerve-racking. This I explain to my passenger, who really expected me to wheel away as soon as the bombs had gone.

227 Squadron reunion, 1988

However, we emerge from the camera run and seeing a bank of heavy cloud just below us and to the west – the approximate direction we must go for home – I dive for it. Once in the cloud I call for a course to steer for the first leg of the return flight. Behind us we can see the cloud lit up from time to time by seach lights or heavy explosions. The navigator gives a course to steer to avoid ground artillery hot spots. A sharp-eyed gunner calls "Coast ahead". At maximum speed we drop down over the coast and settle for home at an exhilarating but definitely not recommended height above the waves. Release from tension must not cause relaxation of concentration, especially at the height above the waves we are flying.

"Land in sight", from the sharpest-eyed look-out. It is the little pier at Skegness. Once again the navigator has brought us accurately to our destination. It is as though the aircraft knows its way home from here. We make our way to our home base and land, tired but gratified to have achieved one more towards our target of thirty trips, and then a rest from operations. Our round trip of six and a half to seven hours has been successful.

"How did you enjoy it?" I ask my passenger. "Very interesting. From time to time I was very frightened".

"So was I. So was I. I always am".

* * *

A tour of operations which, when and if completed, would lead to a less dangerous occupation in the service, consisted of thirty to thirty five operational sorties. Anyone completing more than seventeen sorties was living on borrowed time. This makes the treatment of Jimmy Brown, my first navigator, all the more barbaric. Jimmy expected to be dead in the near future. He could not face up to the prospect. What authority did to him was a disgrace.

227 Squadron reunion, 1988

10

When one has played an exciting and full part in military activity during a war there is little recollection of any other life. Indeed, after nearly sixty years memory only invokes the vividness of dangerous activity. However the importance of what I did and its bearing on my wife Gwen and subsequently my children must be recounted as part of my life story.

I was mobilised for full-time military duty in the early Autumn of 1939. Many people thought that the war would be over by Christmas of the same year. As I was a Territorial soldier I was called up at once; indeed we did not return to civilian life after the summer camp. My employers were amongst those who were convinced that it would be a very short war, and paid my salary to my wife until Christmas, when it became clear that the war was not going to stop suddenly. The phoney war, as it was called, became real; aerial attack in the south of England became imminent; troops were moved into position to fight; some units moved to France; the usual British lack of preparedness was made manifest; there was a shortage of weapons and ammunition; a great deal of equipment dated from the 1918 war. In the meantime night life continued in the wealthier parts of our cities. People paid no heed to Churchill's oft-repeated warnings. Chamberlain had brought back his piece of paper. There would be no *real* war.

Then followed what must have been a time of dreadful uncertainty for wives of servicemen. Employers stopped subsidising employees called up for service. Incomes plummeted. As a private solider I had only a small income, half of which – plus a small allowance for wife and one child – was paid direct to Gwen. It is difficult to contemplate how hard it must have been for the wives of ordinary soldiers to survive on incomes which were no more than a pittance. Fortunately I obtained a commission in the Royal Artillery. My income and my wife's allowance rose quite sharply. Then came the opportunity to learn to fly with the R.A.F. and to add 'flying pay' to my monthly cheque. The tension on Gwen in her struggle to provide a satisfactory life for the children –

Susan, our second daughter, was born in 1941 – must have been intense. When war broke out we had the little bungalow house in Wallington, Surrey, next door to the Dickensons. Emily Dickenson, who was herself childless, became a devoted 'aunt' to our children and a strong support to Gwen, even when we moved house. For we moved from the dangerous environment of Croydon airport to take an inexpensive cottage in Northamptonshire.

I am now conscious of the fact that we were living quite separate lives. Mine was full of new activities, learning new skills and living under the stimulus of facing up to dangers which a few months previously I had not even contemplated. For Gwen there was the daily repetition of the necessary tasks of raising a small family. I suspect that our experiences, which could not in any way be shared, were causing us to grow apart, slowly but inexorably. I was happy that my change of fortune, first by promotion in the Army and then with transfer to the R.A.F, brought with it a steady increase in both my income and in family allowances. But we were less and less together. Training away from home meant that it would be impossible for us to be together for weeks at a time. I felt a strong sense of indebtedness to Gwen that she was able to do such a good job of bringing up our children on her own.

When I had completed training as a flying instructor I was posted to the staff of the flying training school at Spitalgate aerodrome at Grantham in Lincolnshire. We conferred, and agreed to find a house to rent in Grantham, as I would be permitted to live at home while I was there. So we rented a house in Castlegate Road in Grantham. At the end was the grocer's shop of Alderman Roberts. The Alderman was a great force in the land. He was the Mayor of Grantham and the chairman of the local food authority. Gwen found that to complain about any of the services she received from the local shop was futile, as complaints were referred to the local food committee – that is, to Alderman Roberts himself.

One of my recollections of Grantham was much pleasanter than our occasional contretemps with the Alderman. The baker had an arrangement with local ladies that when his ovens were still hot after the day's bread baking was finished they could take their oven trays with meat and vegetables along and, for a very modest charge, have their food cooked in the still hot oven. This was particularly welcome for the rare Sunday joints and for special occasions like Christmas and Easter.

We lived for some time at 26 Castlegate. When I eventually finished my tour at Spitalgate as a flying instructor I went off to be trained as a bomber pilot and was then posted back for operational flying to an emergency aerodrome at Balderton, about ten miles from Grantham. Although I had to live at Balderton, because it was necessary for me to be available for operations which might take off at any time of the day or night, I was able to visit my home and family quite frequently. Deborah, my third daughter, was born in February 1944. I was happy that Gwen seemed to settle down and make a number of friends, especially amongst the wives of the service officers, many of whom had small children of similar ages to our own. It was a social life in which I took little part and, until I became a Wing Commander and C.O. of a squadron, Gwen had little part in my social life. She was, of course, delighted that I was surviving my operational career and I made sure that she should not know any details of those occasions when I confronted any specially dangerous situations. Similarly she was delighted when I was promoted. She loved to visit the squadron as the C.O.'s wife.

When I had been stationed at Montrose I had become very friendly with the skipper of a Royal Navy boat on coastal services off eastern Scotland. One day he asked me whether my wife would like some fish. Most of his crew were keen fishermen; indeed, as far as I can remember they seemed to live happily largely on a diet of fish. I assured him that fresh fish was almost unobtainable in inland towns and villages, so he took Gwen's name and address. A few days later I heard from her that she had received a note from the railway station that there was a parcel of fish for her to collect. Her friend Emily Dickenson was staying, so the two young women went off to the station to collect a whole cod, probably weighing as much as ten or twelve pounds. When they got it back home, they found that they were inadequately equipped with suitable cutting implements. They had to attack it with ordinary, not very sharp, table knives and even – they told me afterwards – with scissors. In those days houses were not equipped with refrigerators, much less freezers, so they had to gorge themselves and the children on massive cod steaks. They were, of course, defeated. The race between eating it all and the onset of putrefaction was lost. A considerable residue was smuggled out to the dustbin. They were, of course, delighted with the bonanza of fresh fish which, at first anyway, they and the children enjoyed.

My staff at Balderton were always delighted to see my pretty wife and children.

We had an arrangement to send an aircraft on a training flight to an aerodrome in the Orkneys. Normal transport to the mainland was practically non-existent in wartime. The islands were full of poultry of all kinds, and eggs by the hundred. So my training aircraft went off with money from the officers, sergeants and other ranks' messes, and came back well-laden with turkeys, chickens, ducks and eggs at bargain prices. All were made available locally where any of the airmen had family and, for the duration of my stay at Balderton, my family dined in royal fashion, frequently using the Castlegate baker's oven.

I did, however, have to issue a friendly rebuke when I discovered that my officer's mess sergeant had supplied a large turkey, for which he made no charge, and made a de luxe stuffing using, so I was told, some twenty eggs. The irony was that by service custom the Commanding Officer made the rounds of the messes on Christmas Day, starting with the airmen and junior N.C.O.s, proceeding to the Sergeants and Warrant Officers, and then to his own Officers' Mess. The convention was – and probably still is – that the C.O. served up Christmas lunch and waited at table. You can be sure that at each mess he was freely regaled with Christmas drinks but, alas, offered nothing to eat. I got home to my house in Castlegate at about six in the evening; rather drunk, but starving.

I found that Gwen and her friend Emily, never having served up anything bigger than a chicken – other than an enormous cod – had fed the children then tackled their twenty pound turkey. First they had cut off a leg each. Well, you do with a chicken, don't you? Then there had to be a goodly portion of white meat from the breast. The stuffing also was delicious, and plentiful. Topped off with a few roast potatoes, it made an adequate meal. When I got home they were still trying, without success, to clean their plates. I look back with some amusement on that turkey. The war was coming to an end. Most of the year we suffered from rationing. Here was plenty and more to spare. A memorable Christmas Day.

* * *

The following April, having expressed my willingness to become a Parliamentary candidate so long as it was in a constituency I could not win, I was elected, in a dramatic by-election, as the Member of Parliament for Chelmsford.

I had almost completed a tour of operations. I had no desire to go back to a 'rest' job, either as an instructor or, worse still, as a desk-bound staff officer. I was delighted to offer myself as a left-wing candidate when a vacancy arose at Chelmsford where the now deceased

Conservative M.P. had had a majority of over sixteen thousand. Although I had to campaign in my one ill-fitting civilian suit I still held my rank. The audiences, which were enormous, asked innumerable questions about bomber operations. We were near enough to London for everybody to be aware of the Blitz. I fear the civilian audiences were much more bloodthirsty than I was. They seemed to hold me personally responsible for the destruction of German cities. My opponent was also an Air Force officer, but not a flying man. The Daily Mirror which, to my embarrassment, adopted my candidature, made much of the fact that 'while Wing Commander Millington was flying through thick flak to bomb Berlin his Tory opponent, Flight Lieutenant Cooke, was signing important documents at the Air Ministry'.

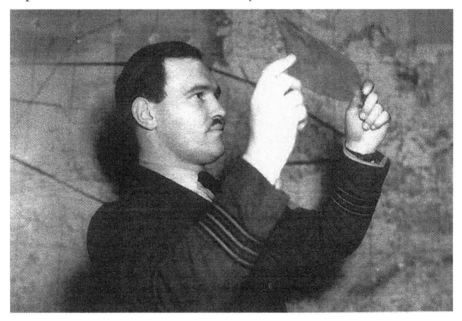

Censored Election photo, 1945

So I was elected Member of Parliament for Chelmsford, and took my seat. There then followed a further sustained period in which Gwen was left unsupported to bring up the children. Four nights a week, if the House of Commons rose on time at 10.30 pm, I did not arrive home until after midnight. There were constituency and party duties to occupy most weekends. For five years, my poor wife was even more deserted than she had been during the war. The process of drifting apart continued unabated. It is difficult to know how an active political life could possibly run compatibly with a domestic life. Although I had not wanted to be elected I could not, in all conscience, neglect my duties as a constituency M.P.

The tradition had been that a seat in the House of Commons was a prerequisite for the sons of wealthy families. When my demobilisation from the R.A.F. came through I had no income other than the Parliamentary salary, which never exceeded £1,000 a year. Part of the pledge I had given was that if elected I would live in the Chelmsford constituency. We found a charming small house at Boreham, three minutes out of Chelmsford on the Colchester road, to which – perforce – I had to return every night. I had an old banger which I had bought from a farmer, who had kept chickens in it throughout the war, for £25. In this decrepit old vehicle I made the hour and a half journey each way to Westminster. It was desperately wearing, although I often gave myself the pleasure of parking it between two Rolls Royces in the House of Commons compound. I was a reluctant and exhausted M.P. The life was far from enjoyable and in my next chapter I will try to give some impressions of the futility of parliamentary democracy which, I am told, is still the best form of government in the world. Perhaps it is better now that M.P.s have private rooms, secretarial allowances and an income from the state which, including allowances (we had none in 1945) amounts to over £51,000 a year.[47] To me and my family it was a period of status accompanied by grinding poverty.

* * *

When I was Member of Parliament for Chelmsford a number of local organisations behaved as though showing courtesy to my wife would bring benefit to the organisation of which she was a member. To give her a leading role in the organisation somehow brought credit and advantage in its wake. Gwen thus became President of the Women's Institute, President of the Mothers' Union and more importantly – importantly because of the leadership role of some of its members – President of the Business and Professional Women's Guild. It is with pleasure that I can recall that Gwen performed all these offices with grace, panache and sensitivity.

---

[47] *In fact £56,358 plus allowances of £18,786 – a total of £75,144 in 2004. (The median income in the UK is £21,000). CM*

Many of the contacts made through these honorifics were quite rewarding. Not least her long and profitable friendship with Vera Smith. Vera was a senior district nurse; an able, well-balanced lady who I never saw lose her temper or show untoward emotion. When we first knew her she was in her mid-forties. For some thirty years she was devoted to our daughters and their mother.

She lived at Thorpe Bay, close to Southend-on-Sea, in a well-appointed house a few hundred yards from the sea. Also living in the same house was her father, a retired Borough Engineer. He had the reputation of being rather too fond of little girls, but his daughter had complete command of the situation.

Vera was so devoted to my girls that when Gwen decided that she must accept the doctor's suggestion that she would most fully recover from the rigours of war by going to Switzerland for a month, Vera agreed that Gwen should take Anne and that she, Vera, would look after the other two. So Gwen and Anne had a month in Switzerland and Vera Smith had the two youngest children, who loved her dearly and whom she in turn dearly loved. For many years Vera was available and willing to look after our children for short or long periods of time. The pleasure she got from the experience was the only reward she sought or was offered.

11

I took my seat, as a Member of Parliament, in the House of Commons on 26th April 1945. I had not foreseen victory.

The war had caused a deferment of electoral activities. The last General Election had been held in 1936, a landslide year for the Tories. Only about forty Labour candidates had been elected. Certainly Chelmsford looked an excellent prospect for a candidate who didn't want to win. I had reached a point in the R.A.F. where I would be rested from operational flying after one more trip. I had no desire to be rested in to a non-flying appointment, nor to return to the comparatively boring world of flying training. I had spent many years as an active political propagandist. After the Churchillian rejection of Beveridge's plan for a more just reorganisation of society when war against Germany was finished, it seemed to me to be necessary that Socialists should be convinced that the biggest enemy after the defeat of Germany and Japan was an unchallenged return to the gross inequalities of pre-war England. They must all do everything possible to prevent a post-war Churchill Government. No service man was permitted to address a political meeting, especially if specifically calling for radical change – unless he or she was an adopted Parliamentary candidate.

There was still a war-time political truce running between the three main political parties (Conservatives, Labour and Liberal). If a vacancy occurred through resignation or the death of a sitting member, the nominee of the party to which he had belonged would not be opposed, The war, clearly, was almost over. The major political parties were advancing their claims for post-war victory.

The Conservative Party based its appeal on the undoubted popularity of Winston Churchill, ignoring the great public interest in the lively debate on the causes of the war and the various answers to the questions: 'What have we been fighting for?' and 'Do we want to return to the kind of society which obtained before the outbreak of war?'

The Labour Party leadership was split almost equally. Half, led by Atlee, Bevin and Morrison, was convinced that only if the wartime coalition was extended for at least a further six months could Labour have any say in post-war development. On the other hand, a big minority led by Aneurin Bevan and Jim Griffiths – slightly less than half the National Executive Committee – wanted the coalition terminated and for each party to fight on its individual policies, based on traditional values and beliefs. In April 1945 the coalition was still inhibiting any major party opposition to the Conservatives when a vacancy occurred in Chelmsford. In 1936 the constituency had had the sixth largest Tory majority in the country. The Labour Party leadership agreed not to fight the Conservative nominee. No such inhibition applied to CommonWealth, which was not signed up to the three party agreement.

This was to be the first election fought on an electoral register which had been revised and brought up to date. In 1936 the Chelmsford electorate had been that of a small, somewhat sleepy market town, surrounded by prosperous agriculture with near-feudal social relationships. By the time of the 1945 by-election the new electoral roll had swamped it with a population laden with engineers, scientists and industrial workers who had been brought into the constituency to man the massive industries which had grown up in Chelmsford and its neighbourhood during war time. I do not think any political leader or commentator had a clear notion that the result of the by-election could be anything but a swingeing Conservative victory. That was certainly my belief, and a strong part of the reason why I accepted nomination.

We in CommonWealth had two things going for us. The first was an unforeseen and virtually unexpressed deep and almost universal desire for change. In and out of the Services powerful voices had for some time been arguing for change. Within the forces the Army Bureau of Current Affairs was producing a stream of discussion pamphlets and organising discussion groups – and even mock Parliaments – to debate the issues being raised. Issues like full employment, education for all according to ability, and economic and employment emancipation for women. On the home front vigorous young educated women were coming forward to organise the changing opinion on a local basis, with the consequent growth not only of membership numbers but also of organisational arrangements in the hands of young people anxious to express their yearning for a changed world after the war. Their hopes for the future were stirred up by some powerful voices. After the evening news[48] J.B.

---

[48] *On the radio: there was no general television service yet.*

Priestley gave a talk about his vision of a possible future. Vernon Bartlett wrote powerfully in the News Chronicle. Other less well-known publicists pursued similar themes. Richard Acland published a Christian Socialist riposte to Hitler's *Mein Kampf.* He called his book *Unser Kampf* (Our Struggle), painting a picture of a caste-free society in which exploitation was impossible and people behaved as well to one another in peace as they had looked out for one another in war.

Acland, Priestley and Bartlett came together to see whether there was a common basis for their beliefs which could take a political form. It was called *Forward March* from a phrase of Priestley's calling for a "forward march of the common people". The original group broke up – too many powerful egos – but Acland gathered up the pieces and eventually formed a political party which he called CommonWealth.

Photo in Election Address

CommonWealth gained strong support, especially from Labour Party members who resented being instructed by their leaders to vote Tory. Unfettered by the electoral truce, CommonWealth was free to run candidates where-ever vacancies occurred. Under the leadership of the National Secretary, Kim Mackay, for the first time in English politics it had developed a method of organising all the people who showed an interest in the party, so that where they ran candidates, members were given tasks. This not only considerably widened the effectiveness of the message but was also supported by a number of workers who, because of their active participation, regarded the party and its message as very specifically *their* party, and *their* message.

The writ for the by-election was moved and polling day fixed for seventeen days later. The Air Ministry stopped my service pay for those seventeen days. This, to a young married man with a wife and three children, was a cruel blow. Although I do not think I went out of my way to tell anybody of my plight, one of my industrialist supporters, appropriately named Mr Good, presented me with a cheque covering the amount of the stoppage.

It became clear from the size and enthusiasm of the meetings that we had at least a chance of doing well. Traditional trade union and Labour Party members and supporters reacted adversely to their leadership, which gave them explicit instructions to vote for the Tory candidate. We filled the local cinemas with uninhibited Socialist messages. To my amazement mention of Winston Churchill, instead of being the crowd winner the Conservatives expected, was often greeted with boos – especially if associated with his often quoted opposition to what is now called Social Security and the Welfare State.[49]

The names of Atlee, Morrison and Ernie Bevin were greeted with enthusiasm. The industrial workers wanted change. CommonWealth was offering a stronger lead for change than the National Executive Committee of the Labour Party. So I enjoyed warm support from all the forces which were the traditional mainstay of Labour candidates. Gradually it occurred to us that we could win. Our message of the last few mass meetings was not one of policy. "We are going to win", I announced. "Come in on the winning side and make it an historical victory". They did. It was. I took my seat in the House of Commons on 26th April 1945.

* * *

I cannot resist commenting on a typically unfortunate turn of events. Most people coming out of the forces at the end of the war were given counselling and training, if required, in a civilian occupation. Those

---

[49] Extract from a Churchill election broadcast on June 1st 1945:

"Socialism is, in its essence, an attack not only upon British enterprise, but upon the right of the ordinary man or woman to breathe freely without having a harsh, clumsy, tyrannical hand clapped across their mouths and nostrils."

who clearly – in the eyes of Authority – had no need, were not approached. If I had had a profession in which I was securely established before being called to military service; if I had been a large shareholder in a successful family business; if I had been a qualified member of a profession which was desperately short of active members, such as teaching; or if there had been any other reason to presume that the State was not called upon to give me guidance or training, I would be passed over being given any kind of help. I can only presume that the people who made the decision as to whether I would have been helped by training or advice were of the opinion that to have been elected a Member of Parliament would carry me forward into some magic world of civilian life success. I was not offered any training, advice or help. It is to be presumed that I was of the order of people who gave advice, whether sought or not. So I missed out on the kind of help that was available to most ex-service folk at the time of demobilisation.

I took my seat, first in a by-election, and then in the General Election that followed a few weeks later, as the Member of Parliament for Chelmsford.[50] A number of my neighbours in the county of Essex, with whom I had been on visiting terms as a Wing Commander in the R.A.F., and therefore a member or supporter of the social status quo, immediately cut off all communication. It was not hard for me. On the whole I did not like the county set, especially the ladies to whom I was a traitor to my class. It was, however, hard on Gwen.

We had bought a little house in the village of Boreham, a couple of miles out of Chelmsford. It was a small four-bedroomed clapboard house with a big kitchen with an Aga, a good dining room and a sitting room leading onto a conservatory. There was a fair-sized garden with a barn-like outbuilding in which we kept chickens. In it, apart from flowers, we were able to grow vegetables and soft fruit – most welcome when one has a growing family. The children were settled in a Chelmsford primary school. Gwen, as the local M.P.'s wife, found high office in the local and county Mother's Union and Women's Institutes. Except that money was, as always in my first marriage, disastrously short, life proceeded quite happily – leaving me, the reluctant elected

---

[50] The by-election took place on April 26th 1945. Voting in the General Election was on July 5th (the count was on July 26th to allow time for the votes of those serving overseas to arrive). General Election result: Labour 393 seats, Conservatives 213, Liberals 12, CPBB 2 and CommonWealth 1.

representative, to make my entry into the House of Commons.

My first impressions were quite startling. One must remember that there had been no General Election since 1936: all electoral activities had been suspended during the Second World War. I took my seat as the youngest member of a House of Commons that was showing signs of decrepitude. There were, I seem to remember, two or three invalid chairs, three or four members who were obliged to support themselves on crutches, and even one or two who had to aid ailing hearing with clearly visible hearing aids.

One of the first sitting members to greet me in a friendly way was Edith Summerskill.[51] She herself was younger than the average age of the members. She realised that I would not be receiving the support offered to the new M.Ps of the major parties, in the way of documents and a guided tour of the building (in which the location of restaurants, cafeterias, barbers' shops, bathrooms, library and committee rooms was pointed out). It was a great kindness which was – and is – much appreciated. When I commented on the decrepit appearance of some of the members, Edith gave as her explanation the fact that the House of Commons gave a fairly precise and faithful representation in miniature of the country as a whole. Nearly 20 per cent had some physical disability and, as I would discover by observation, 27 per cent were E.S.N.[52] or otherwise mentally incapacitated.

I made friends easily. Amongst my good friends was the Member for Broxtowe, Nottinghamshire, a lively journalist with a wicked sense of humour. Seymour Cocks was one of the cripples I had observed. He only had one leg. He had been in a serious accident when young, and had a leg amputated. He managed very ably with an artificial leg and crutches. He was unmarried, and a great favourite of Gwen, who was delighted and flattered to be called Nephertiti. (Personally I could never see the similarity but in the mid-forties there was a considerable Egyptian art cult; Nephertiti was not only a Queen but, according to the cognoscenti, one of the most beautiful women of the ancient world.) My children too were delighted with a kindly and generous 'uncle', who became a frequent weekend visitor at Boreham. A favourite past-time was to

---

[51] Edith Summerskill: 1901–1980. A doctor. She was an MP from 1938 –1961 (Parliamentary Secretary at the Ministry of Food 1945–1950, and Minister of National Insurance 1950–51), and made a life peer in 1961.

[52] E.S.N. – Educationally Sub Normal.

volunteer to take Seymour up an early morning cup of tea, in order to look with awed amazement at his trousers, carefully placed over the back of the chair, still containing the artificial leg.

In his constituency his sense of humour took a more raunchy turn. At election times he designed special posters for an area of his constituency known, because of the political nature of many of its inhabitants, as Little Moscow. His favourite election poster, reserved exclusively for this neighbourhood, carried the slogan: 'The ladies of little Moscow know how to put Cocks in'.[53]

Someone I was not so fond of was one of three Labour members elected in the General Election who came from Scotland Road, Liverpool. Her name was Bessie Braddock. She was a powerfully built 45 year old, working class and motherly. [54]

Part of new members' briefing, usually given by a long-serving member of the Whips' office, covered the process known as 'catching the Speaker's eye'. In point of fact, members wishing to intervene in a forthcoming debate would present themselves at the office of the Speaker's Chief Secretary. They would then argue that they had a special contribution to make which qualified them to be called. One might have been the chair of the appropriate committee when a member of a local authority; another might have just come back from Outer Mongolia which gave him a special knowledge of the problems facing Peru; a third might have been a Civil Servant before being elected an M.P. – this was a category much favoured by the Speaker's Clerk who was, after all, a Civil Servant himself.

This information was then given in advance to the Speaker, who planned out a balanced debate, giving opportunity for the passing of specialist knowledge, or for the confrontation of conflicting points of view. It is rumoured that when Bessie Braddock was informed of this procedure, she riposted in a very loud voice: "Nobody is going to tell *me* when I can speak or not". It is interesting to note that she finished her membership of Parliament, a period of some twenty four years, a very tame, orthodox and well-behaved Member.

Throughout my membership of the House of Commons I was

---

[53] Seymour Cocks was a Labour MP 1945 -1953

[54] "Battling" Bessie Braddock (1899-1970) was Labour MP for Liverpool Exchange for 24 years. She once famously told Churchill: "Winston, you're drunk!". He replied "Bessie, you're ugly. But in the morning I shall be sober".

aware that more than one member regarded this method of determining who would be called to speak as not in the full spirit of democratic debate. It gave excessive power to the Speaker and his staff and made a farce of the fact that whenever a member sat down on completion of a contribution, every other member who would like to be called leapt to his feet, sometimes waving an order paper and often calling out "Mr Speaker, Sir!" in a loud voice, as though already beginning a speech. Such attempts to catch the Speaker's eye were ignored, and the next person to join in the debate was called upon by the Speaker after checking his prepared list. Amongst those who were most determined in seeking a change in this procedure were two Labour members who always sat together on the front bench, below the gangway, on the Government side.

Sidney Silverman, the smallest member of the House, was a tiny, white-haired Manchester Jew, a very able debater and one of the sharpest wits in Parliament. Next to him sat Dick Stokes. Dick was as big as Sidney was small. The small one had a high-pitched voice, his big friend a deep voice that matched his frame. They were not in agreement in their interpretation of Labour policy. Sidney was a man of the left, Dick of the right. What they did have in common was a deep hostility to the traditional method of catching the Speaker's eye. So they planned a campaign. First of all, ignoring the convention of having first consulted the Speaker's Clerk, they leapt to their feet as each Member who had been 'called' completed what he had to say. The pantomime was repeated, but in every case some other member was named. Eventually, after several hours without failing to leap up whenever there was a gap between speakers, all without avail, Dick rose on a point of order. If a Member rises on a point of order, the rules of the House oblige the Speaker to listen to him.

"What is your point of order?" asked the Speaker.

"My honourable friend and I have each a valuable contribution to make to this debate. In accordance with the rules of the House we have indicated our desire to speak as each prior speaker sits down. May I seek your guidance, Mr Speaker? What – apart from rising to one's feet – must one do to catch your eye?"

The Speaker was clearly too wily to describe what in fact had to happen, namely that the aspirant had to arrange it with his Clerk.

"The traditional method is that you should rise to your feet at the conclusion of every speech. So far I have not noticed you."

Part two of the plan was then brought into play. Sidney and Dick took out of their pockets flamboyant silk hankies and scarves. These they trailed from jacket pockets and wound round their necks. Sidney tied one over his hair in the supposed fashion of a pirate. The next break in the debate led to another Member being called. This went on for some time. Then Sidney rose on a point of order. The result was the same. They were both ignored.

At the end of the session they were invited to a meeting in the Speaker's house. A compromise arrangement was made that was kept secret in case it became the normal way for all members to indicate their desire to speak.[55]

* * *

During the first few weeks of this Parliament, servicemen who had been elected in the General Election and had not yet been demobilised were expected to attend in uniform. A few weeks into the session I was awarded the Distinguished Flying Cross. This was announced in the morning newspapers so I was obliged to sew the appropriate piece of coloured ribbon on to my uniform. I am the first to admit that I am an inadequate seamstress. My strip of ribbon was fractionally too wide. It did not accord exactly with regulations. As I walked into the Palace of Westminster I was approached by a Tory M.P. whom I knew to have been an R.A.F. military police officer, with the rank of Squadron Leader, also probably not yet demobilised. He was in civilian clothes and came up to me with a hand in a trouser pocket.

"You are improperly dressed", he said, "Your D.F.C. ribbon is too wide".

He was, I think, not expecting my reaction.

"If you are talking to me as an R.A.F. officer: stand to attention; take your hand out of your trouser pocket and address a senior officer as 'Sir'. If you are talking as a fellow Member of Parliament, mind your business and bugger off."

He must have felt that he was in M.P. mode. He buggered off.

* * *

Of the leading members of the House, the two who impressed

---

[55] Sidney Silverman was MP for Nelson 1935-1968. He was a leading campaigner for the abolition of the death penalty. Richard Stokes was MP for Ipswich.

me most were John Strachey and Aneurin Bevan.

John lived in my constituency. He was a senior member of the party, a Cabinet Minister and a very helpful friend. Occasionally Gwen and I dined with him and his wife, who lived only a few miles away from us. I shared with those who knew him some astonishment that Strachey had been recognised by Atlee and appointed a minister. At first, possibly because he had been a Squadron Leader during the war, he was answerable in the House of Commons for R.A.F. affairs. His Civil Servants produced for him the drafts of the speeches he was to make, usually – indeed probably always – after Ministerial discussion. Each speech was then vetted by the Minister who had the right to make small amendments. Most of the speeches made by the Air Ministers in the 1945 Parliament were technical statements to do with the suggested running down of squadrons and other manpower cuts. John used to add a final paragraph, giving his personal thanks to the men and women who had fought so bravely against Nazism, and expressing the hope that they would be made available to continue the fight against Facism where ever it might appear. The speech always came back with the final paragraph deleted. His Permanent Secretary sought to explain that a statement on the future of the R.A.F. was not a proper vehicle for the personal political feelings of the Minister. The dispute was taken to the Prime Minister, who supported the civil servant. Strachey was removed and transferred to the Ministry of Food.[56]

My total admiration for Aneurin Bevan can perhaps best be expressed by an incident in the Second Reading debate on the National Health Service bill. Nye was notorious for the fact that whatever he was discussing, in the House of Commons or on a platform outside, he had no need of notes. He did not have to read his speeches. He had a slight stammer which, it was held by some, was used with great skill to give himself a split second or two for thought.

I was present when the Conservative government which succeeded Atlee was introducing itself in the House. The new Secretary of State for Wales was an Englishman. The Prime Minister sought to justify the appointment of this particular Englishman on the grounds that

---

[56] John Strachey 1901–1963. Author of *The Menace of Fascism* (1933) and *The Theory and Practice of Socialism* (1936). In 1936 he joined with Victor Gollancz and Harold Laski to form the Left Book Club. Secretary for Air (1945-46), Minister of Food (1946-50) and Secretary of State for War (1950-51).

he had done many things in his public life which had affected Wales favourably. That, in fact, he was very popular in Wales and his appointment would be welcome. At which point Aneurin got to his feet.

"P...p...popular! You say he is popular! Let me reassure you that in the mountains and valleys of the p..p...p...principality his name is abom... abom... abom...EXECRATED!" The last word spat out with vigour and passion. He may have intended 'execrated' all along. It just had more power after he had obtained the sympathy of his audience who, friend and foe alike, had been willing him to say 'abominated'.

The real greatness of the man was shown at the opening debate introducing the National Health Service Bill. After a fascinating philosophical introduction on the history of health provision in the United Kingdom, he then proceeded to go through the bill clause by clause, describing the details, giving way to questioners and answering what it was they had interrupted for. He had been going without a fault for over an hour. It was a very long bill. An enquiring voice asked permission to pose a question. Nye sat down to indicate his willingness to hear the question.

"I see no mention of the future of domiciliary nursing. Will the Minister tell us if he has any plans for this service?" Without apparently pausing for breath, Nye was on his feet.

"This is all discussed in Clause 278 of the first appendix. When we reach that point I will happily refer to it".

Not unnaturally everyone with a copy of the Bill turned to Appendix 1, Clause 278. There it was – Auxiliary Nursing.

In a later administration Nye was promoted to the third great office of state – Foreign Secretary. His political friends were agog to hear some radical approach indicating a new mind in the Foreign Office. It was, though, a sad moment to hear our radical, left wing hero make a speech which justified the British possession of atomic weapons with the weary cliché, "I have no intention of going naked into the conference chamber". No qualifications. No Welsh wizardry to explain what was a volte face in the crudest terms against a lifetime of querying the moral justification of possessing the Bomb.[57]

---

[57] Aneurin Bevan 1897-1960. MP for Ebbw Vale 1929-1960. Shadow Foreign Secretary 1956. It was at the 1957 Labour Party Conference that he spoke against unilateral nuclear disarmament, arguing "It would send a British Foreign Secretary naked into the conference-chamber".

12

When a General Election is in the offing the managers of the major political parties produce lists of sitting members and adopted candidates. It is in the party's interest to contest every seat, even those which cannot be won. For example, the Conservative Party always contests the mining or former mining districts, the steel towns and the other constituencies where the solid tradition of vast Labour majorities makes the Tory challenge to win quite impossible. Similarly the Labour Party always puts up candidates in the rural areas where the political traditions are solidly Conservative. There are two motives at least for this apparent waste of time, money and effort.

The first is that every party wishes to register the highest possible number of votes, taking into consideration the returns of all the constituencies. From this can readily be calculated each party's share of the national vote expressed as a percentage of the whole. Let me arbitrarily take a specific example. In 1948 the state of the parties in the House of Commons was as follows.

			% of 640 seats	*total of approx 23.5m votes cast*
Labour	394		70.5%	12,250,000
Conservative	191		30%	7,005,000
Lib.Nats	13	)		
Liberal	10	)	8.5%	4,245,000
Others	28	)		
Vacancies	4	)		

With only half the total national vote, Labour secured over 70% of the seats; the Conservatives with 7 million votes had less than 30% of the seats. All the others between them polled nearly four and a half million votes but had less than 9% of the seats. This outcome is widely defended by the two political parties which hope to come out of a General Election with something like the 1945 - 50 Labour Party position.

Every party before a General Election will prophecy great success at the polls for itself. The second motive for fighting every seat is that success does sometimes happen. A landslide victory, such as the one that gave one party 70% of the seats for nearly 50% of the votes, is welcomed by the winning side as proof that the first past the post system takes cognisance of regional variations and ultimately represents a most democratic measurement of the national will. The losing side, whatever they may have said in the past when they had scored a landslide victory, condemn the fact that half the electorate is represented by candidates for whom they have not voted. Those who favour a system of proportional representation point out, as the results of each General Election are declared, that in their view it would be more fair and democratic if each party were to be allocated a number of seats proportionate to their nationally polled numbers.

It is no part of my brief to argue the two conflicting cases at this point. I would point out that the crude form of proportional representation would eliminate the elements of local knowledge and identification of Members of Parliament with specific constituencies and specific constituents.

* * *

The determination of the major political parties to contest as many seats as possible, in order to record the highest possible figure of support throughout the country, gives rise to some remarkable candidates who are permitted to stand in unwinnable seats. All political parties are consortia of elements which may more or less share the same philosophy of government.

The Labour Party still contains a significant number of traditional members. They are mainly Socialist in economic theory and heavily committed to the welfare of the poor, the weak and the needy. They represent a strong lobby for health and education and, their opponents claim, are weak on immigration. On the other hand, the leadership of the Labour Party which has emerged since 1979 represents a very untraditional willingness to compromise with the worlds of finance and big business. The Conservative Party cannot make up its mind whether it is the party which at all costs must defend the countryside against intrusion. It is also very confused about Britain's role in Europe. Leading figures in the Conservative Party make statements which regularly contradict previous statements made by their colleagues. Neither party can afford to cold-shoulder a significant group, especially if such a group was a source of strong electoral support and all-the-year-round financial assistance. It is significant that both the major political parties are in dire straits financially. The clarity of the message of each is obscured by the need to cast words of comfort to minority groups. And the loyalty of these groups is rewarded by the endorsement of some of their number to be Parliamentary candidates.

In theory the political leaders in each locality are responsible for the adoption and nomination of their Parliamentary candidates. Their decision is sent to Party HQ, where it is either ratified or challenged. In an 'unwinnable' constituency the candidate, probably with strong local connections and forty years of faithful service on the local committee, will be put forward. The honour of being a parliamentary candidate, even in an impossible situation, is given as a reward to the faithful servant. Party Head Office, glad to have any candidate, especially one who could be expected to pick up a reasonable quantity of local votes, has no difficulty in endorsing the candidate.

For the most part strong candidates vie to obtain nomination for a good winnable seat. When a leading or well-established celebrity politician, like Tony Benn, announces his intention not to contest the next election there is a move amongst the ambitious (who may be sitting M.P.s in marginal seats, or who may have failed in a difficult marginal constituency in the last election) to come forward and seek nomination to fill the vacancy. Sometimes, in order to make room for a senior politician to stand for a safe seat, pressure may be brought to bear to persuade the sitting member to apply for the stewardship of the Chiltern Hundreds.[58] It could be that the sitting Member resigns out of loyalty to the interests of the Party. More likely, alas, resignation is secured by the promise of an honour or an appointment. It is therefore possible for party managers to fill the candidate lists for General Elections with most

---

[58] 'Under a Resolution of the House of 2 March 1623, Members of Parliament cannot directly resign their seat. Death, disqualification, elevation to the Peerage, dissolution or expulsion are the only causes by which a Member's seat can be vacated. Therefore a Member wishing to resign has to go through the process of applying for a paid office of the Crown which automatically disqualifies the Member from holding a seat in the House of Commons. There are two such offices: Crown Steward and Bailiff of the Chiltern Hundreds and the Manor of Northstead.' *Extract from the House of Commons website – which also lists the 52 M.P.s who have been appointed to the Chiltern Hundreds or the Manor of Northstead Stewardships between 1970 and June 2004.*

of their leadership figures fitted out with constituencies which will ensure that they are safely elected, plus a fair range of reasonable candidates who, after a good fight, have more than a little chance being elected plus a rump of make-the-numbers-up candidates who are not expected to win.

The 'system' usually works but, from time to time, it is shot to pieces by a party's landslide victory. Senior party managements rarely anticipate the possibility of such a victory.

The Attlee Labour Party of 1945, led by Bevin, Morrison and Dalton, was so sure that Labour could not win the impending General Election that it was proposed that the electoral truce, which they had entered into with the Tories during the War, should continue for at least another six months, and that the coalition should persist until at least six months after hostilities against German and Japan had ceased. The timid prognosis was that the Labour Party, fighting under its own banner, could not possibly succeed against the immense popularity of Winston Churchill : 'the man who had won the war'. Whatever the Conservatives thought – and I suspect that most of them were completely taken in by the Churchill myth – it took the Chelmsford by-election of April 1945 to change these views.

CommonWealth was a genuinely left-wing political party. It advocated a socialist economic policy, eschewing the pre-war stranglehold on the one hand of the unions and on the other of banks, insurance companies and other big business. There was a strong element of Christianity, largely through the personal leadership of Sir Richard Acland. It led to direct support from a fair number of bishops and other leading churchmen. It enabled the party to justify slogans like – 'If it is morally wrong, it cannot be politically right'. Perhaps above all it was a political force unhampered by affiliation with non-party political bodies. Many people had been put off from supporting the Labour Party because of the power and influence of the Trade Union movement. Similarly many who felt a strong emotional pull towards free enterprise and all it entailed were discouraged from giving emotional support to the Conservative Party. However, the War came to an end. The startling Chelmsford by-election result in April encouraged the Labour Party to withdraw from the wartime coalition and to prepare for the first General Election for nine years.

It was Aneurin Bevan who told me that the hierarchy of leaders in the National Executive Committee of the Labour Party wanted to sustain the coalition for at least six months, but that the result at

Chelmsford showed that an unknown politician, preaching an ethical Socialist policy, belonging to a party unmentionably small, could defeat a Government candidate supported by both Conservative and Labour parties. The coalition broke up. In the General Election that followed, the Labour Party achieved a landslide victory. The leader of the Labour Party, Clement Atlee, was sent for by the King and instructed to form a government.

It is said that the two high offices of state that the sovereign can oppose are Prime Minister and Foreign Secretary. Foreign Secretary because, constitutionally, he speaks for the sovereign abroad. Ernie Bevin was to have been Chancellor of the Exchequer and Hugh Dalton Foreign Secretary in the original list submitted to the King. Hugh Dalton was a large academic with an enormous voice. He was a Ph.D., and loved to surround himself with admiring students to whom he boomed out his opinions. It was during this short period, when everyone knew that Hugh had been put forward as Foreign Secretary, that he was sitting in the House of Commons giving his opinions on a variety of subjects in his usual very loud voice. Seymour Cocks paused in passing.

"There is one cardinal principle of Labour foreign policy that will be sustained if you become Foreign Secretary".

"And what is that?" demanded Dalton.

"No more secret treaties!" replied Cocks, as he limped off.

Hugh Dalton was the son of a former chaplain of Windsor Castle. He had been brought up with the children of King George V. They had been overwhelmed as children by his physical size and his enormous voice. When Dalton's name was submitted to King George VI the King refused his approval. No way was he going to be represented abroad by the man who, as a boy, had bullied him by his overwhelming presence. So Attlee had to make a change at the top of his list of ministers. Ernest Bevin, the dock-worker from Rotherhithe, became Foreign Secretary and Hugh Dalton, Chancellor of the Exchequer. Thus the memory of a childhood hate put into power in the Foreign Office a Minister who had spent his life combating the influence of the Communist Party in the trade union movement. It appeared that Ernie Bevin viewed the Soviet Union as a renegade branch of the Transport and General Workers Union and must be opposed at all costs. The Cold War had begun.

Dalton did not last long in the Treasury. He had unorthodox views on the conduct of national finances. For example he preached, loudly, the virtues of cheap money. If the interest rate were low, industry and commerce would borrow more and speed up industrial recovery. Unfortunately if the interest rate is low, although more people want to borrow, fewer want to lend. Under a short regime of low interest rates, investment and commercial lending stagnated. Recovery came to a standstill. Clearly the Chancellor of the Exchequer had made a major error in judgement. Dalton must go. He went.

Happily for Prime Minister Attlee the appointment of Sir Stafford Cripps as Ambassador to Moscow came to an end. He was found a safe constituency, Bristol Central, and appointed Chancellor of the Exchequer.

It is perhaps difficult for anybody with an earned six-figure income as a top lawyer to envisage what is meant by austerity. For most of his fellow-citizens in post war Britain, all life was austere. Cripps decreed that to save money on the importation of cloth, particularly cotton, the clothes ration should be reduced. As children are smaller than adults, and their clothes are correspondingly smaller, they had less need of clothing coupons. He proposed therefore to cut children's clothing allowance. He was frankly astounded when two facts of life were pointed out to him. The first, that children grow out of their clothes and need constantly to be fitted out. And secondly that parents, particularly mothers, seek to help out in this dilemma by using their own coupons for their children.

I have no doubt that Cripps was a good man. For example, when John Driscoll, headmaster of a school in Stratford, East London, was at the point where children were being allocated to temporary foster parents away from the danger of being bombed in cities, he was astonished to be confronted with an elegant young woman, who exclaimed:

"Father says we will take four badly behaved girls".

"Can you tell me who 'father' is?"

"Sir Stafford Cripps".

John Driscoll thought for a moment and said, "Will he take three badly behaved boys and a headmaster?"

So it was arranged. The staff of a slum East End school held their staff meetings in the study of the former Ambassador to Moscow. Cripps politely asked if he could sit in on such meetings whenever he was at home. Permission was, of course, freely granted. After anguished debate among teachers who would all have liked their own way, their host would sum up, pointing out their areas of disagreement and making gentle compromise suggestions. In the end agreement would be reached, all the teachers present being quite convinced that they had got their own way.

Attlee had in his Cabinet Herbert Morrison, Deputy Prime Minister and Lord President of the Council; Ernest Bevin, Foreign Secretary and Stafford Cripps, who he had appointed Chancellor of the Exchequer. It would have been impossible for him to ignore the Conference favourite Aneurin Bevan, who was keen to introduce a National Health Service. Others whose appointment fulfilled the need to gratify powerful groups in the party included James Chuter Ede, Arthur Creech Jones and Philip Noel Baker, who were appointed to the offices of Home Secretary, Secretary of State for the Colonies and Secretary of State for Commonwealth Relations respectively. The young Harold Wilson, who was making a name for himself in the Civil Service, went to the Board of Trade.

At the time of Attlee's Cabinet-making the Government of the U.S.A. showed its animosity to the election of a leftish government in the U.K. They called in all the loans made during World War Two under the lease-lend agreements and used their influence to get the International Monetary Fund and other bodies which they dominated to do the same. British overseas investments had to be liquidated. The country was on the verge of bankruptcy. It was, on an international scale, like lending someone the money which they spent on armaments that you sold them to defend the world against a common enemy then, when the enemy was defeated, to demand that the recipient should sell off all assets to repay the debt. Rarely has there been a more outstanding example of a callous attempt to bankrupt an ally because of dislike of the government elected by the people. I have little doubt that if Winston Churchill had won the 1945 General Election, American terms would have been much more generous and cooperative. So we entered a period of post-war austerity that was much less tolerable than the austerity of the war. During a war people can be seen to be cooperating against a common enemy. After the General Election of 1945, with the mainly Conservative press attributing all economic ills to the government, hardship – including continued food and clothing rationing – was difficult for the populace in general to understand. They thought we had just won a war. They didn't realise that we were paying for it, and for the foolhardiness of an electorate in putting a Labour government into office.

One of the most delightful characters in the new government was George Tomlinson, the Minister of Education. He was a roly-poly Lancastrian, modest and a man of great common sense and high good humour. In those days university graduates had two votes, one in the constituency in which they lived, and the other in the election of an M.P.

to represent the university from which they had graduated. The M.P. for Belfast University was a certain Professor D.L. Savory. He immediately launched a virulent attack upon the appointment of George Tomlinson. How could a man who had left school at fourteen possibly direct the educational policy of the nation? It was pointed out – not by Mr Tomlinson, but by his many vigorous defenders – that whereas there was no record of Professor Savory giving up one hour of his life in doing unpaid work for education, George Tomlinson had devoted all his spare time as a trade unionist and as a Socialist to voluntary work on local, county and national bodies aiming to increase opportunities for higher education for many more than the privileged few who traditionally were so favoured.

In the austere days of 1945 the newly appointed Minister of Education was travelling unrecognised in a first class carriage. He was surrounded by businessmen who were discussing the shocking times they were compelled to live in because of this terrible government. Unable to keep silent any longer, George drew attention to himself by unbuttoning his coat and turning down the top of his trousers to reveal his underpants.

"Don't worry yourselves", he said. "I am not going to commit indecent exposure. I want to show you that I am wearing the very best Sea Island cotton underpants. I spent over thirty years of my life making them, but I was never able to afford to buy a pair for myself. Now I can. Thanks to the government which is pledged to do much more for the working man than give him a choice of better underwear."

"Who the hell are you?" one of his fellow travellers interjected.

"I am a Minister in the dreadful government you are all running down so heatedly. You may never get another chance to put your questions directly to a member of the government. From now to the end of the journey I am willing to answer any points you might like to put to me."

After the first few minutes, in which they all wanted to shout at once, they settled down to a useful – and eventually friendly – discussion.

* * *

Amongst the other appointments which started off in a shower of vituperative reaction was that of Emmanuel Shinwell as Secretary of State for War. Manny was a Manchester Jew who had been a conscientious objector in World War One. He had in fact gone to prison for his convictions. It was therefore a surprising choice.

The custom for years had been for the Imperial War Council to meet, under the chairmanship of the Secretary of State, not more often than once a month. Shinwell introduced a regime of two meetings a month. The first was in the traditional form. Senior officers came in uniform. The questions were framed by the Chief of Staff. Each question was posed to the general officer responsible for the policy or practice being queried. On the whole, professional criticism was minimal. Generals do not attack one another. This meeting the new Secretary of State continued. However, he added a second monthly meeting: civilian clothes, comfortable armchairs, pints of beer or other beverages. The agenda was written by the Secretary of State. No question was submitted for answer direct to the general officer responsible. It was put to another officer of similar rank but no direct responsibility. Frequently a fresh approach revealed an entirely new slant on a problem. The informal meetings, which at first were resented as an unwelcome breach of tradition, were eventually eagerly looked forward to. Senior officers were no longer constantly on the defensive – which was the tenor of the formal meetings.

In the early days after the War there were so many problems connected with the Services, demobilisation, pensions and so on that every town had a Ministry of Defence office. I can remember taking a constituent's query to my local M.O.D. office in Chelmsford, The query was dealt with by a comparatively young Army officer. I was so impressed by the logic and clarity of the answer that I mentioned it to Shinwell the next time I saw him in the House. He was delighted, not only with what I had to say but also that I had taken the trouble to say it to him.

"It is very gratifying", he said, "to have confirmation that the systems of communication I have sought to instil have penetrated and that a young local captain gives basically the same response as if you had written to the Minister".

* * *

Earlier in this chapter I mentioned that Professor Savory was M.P. for Belfast University. During the 1945 - 50 Parliament the practice of dual votes for graduates was abolished. 'One man, one vote, in one constituency' very properly became the rule. The one exception to the general rule that the university vote was on the whole wasted was the

Oxford University representative, comic writer and wit A.P. Herbert.

When a member wished to introduce a Private Member's Bill, as opposed to a Government Bill, he brought it typed and tied up with red ribbon and ceremoniously 'laid it on the table'. The document was then taken to the appropriate committee of the house. The decision as to who would be permitted to present his bill for a Second Reading was settled by lottery. Sometimes M.P.s would allow their names to go into the lottery even if they hadn't a bill to present. Other M.P.s would then seek to use their option by persuasion or some other device.

Sir Alan Herbert had been fortunate enough to have succeeded in introducing a Private Member's Bill. I think it was 'The Bill of Divorcement' – or is that the name of the play he wrote on the same subject?[59] He was a lively member of the House, always jumping up on points of order to challenge some traditional practice. In particular he thought bringing in bills and going through the process of 'laying them on the table' was archaic and should be exposed as farce. One day he came into the House and took his habitual seat down below the gangway on the Opposition side on the front bench. In his arms he had a bundle of red taped bills. At the appropriate time he rose to his feet on a point of order.

"I do not waste time laying my many private member's bills on the table", he roared. "I cast them on the floor".

At which he hurled his little bundle of bills to the ground. They must have been badly tied. They unrolled. They were all blank.

* * *

A less happy story of this period is that of John Belcher, M.P. for Sowerby. John, right up to election to Parliament, had been a railway clerk. To all accounts he was meticulous in his work and honest as the day is long. He was appointed Parliamentary Secretary to the Board of Trade. At that time shortages in many industrial and commercial enterprises were subject to Government permission by licensing. The licensing authority was the Board of Trade. The Parliamentary Secretary was held to have considerable influence over the issue of licence certificates. He therefore became a target for those who would exploit his position if possible. One such was a man who operated on the outskirts

---

[59] *It was the Matrimonial Clauses Bill (1937) – which liberalised the divorce laws.*

of legitimate business; a Mr Fixit. John met this man, probably at a Board of Trade function. They became friendly. Their wives met. Mrs Belcher was given a present of two pairs of silk stockings. John was offered two bottles of whisky, which he declined.

A national newspaper got hold of the story, which started as the wife of the Parliamentary Secretary to the Board of Trade receiving presents which were at the time in short supply, developing into allegations of wholesale corruption. Horrified by these allegations, John Belcher resigned his office at the Board of Trade and then his seat in the House of Commons. An internal enquiry exonerated him of any offence or breach of the rules, but he felt shame that he should ever have been considered as one who might be approached to take a bribe. He went back to selling tickets on the railway, but died tragically soon after that.

* * *

Naomi Mitchison, the author, was married to G.R. (Dick) Mitchison, M.P. for Kettering. Her brother was the famous scientist, J.B.S. Haldane. They were invited to Tom Driberg's wedding, of whom more anon. Tom was a rather precious medievalist and it was decided to have the whole service based upon pre-sixteenth century rituals, except that a modern musician composed an exit piece in fifteenth century style but based on the melody of the Red Flag. Only two churches in London could offer the esoteric ritual the occasion called for. One was already fully engaged on the day set aside for the nuptials. The other was a tiny church in Soho. Invitations to the wedding were limited, but even so it was expected that the church would be very full. The secret inevitably leaked out. Tom was a popular Member of Parliament. His constituency was less than twenty miles away. Buses were hired. Parties were arranged and, well before the time due for the wedding, the church was full and the street outside was a milling mass of Maldon voters.

Into this melee appeared Naomi Mitchison, her brother and her husband. They forced themselves into the church just sufficiently to be able to see the tops of the heads of the principals. J.B.S. Haldane was fascinated by the medieval ritual. He managed to find a slightly raised area from which he could see better. Suddenly Naomi heard a match strike. Haldane had filled and was lighting his pipe.

"You can't smoke in here. You're in church", she whispered.

"Am I?" he asked. "I was investigating an important socio-historical phenomenon. I always light a pipe when I am investigating. It helps concentration".

The Driberg wedding served his purpose. As a married man he could not be a homosexual. There was nothing to prevent his elevation to the peerage. He later became Lord Bradwell.[60]

* * *

'Chips' Channon and Viscount Iveagh were both members of the Guinness clan. They were both M.P.s. They both drove the latest and most luxurious Rolls Royces. One day they had parked side by side in the Commons car park. When they came out to go home, draped across the front of the two Rolls was a banner – *Guinness is Good For You.*

* * *

One of the leading principles of the P.N.E.U[61] system of education is that children should be exposed to the highest forms of literature from a very early age. Anne was perhaps five and a half when she was presented with a shortened version of Milton's *Il Penseroso.* One section is in praise of Italy. It contains the interesting statement that parts of Italy are so fertile that the apple trees flower and fruit twice in a year. Ivor Thomas was a junior minister in the Atlee 1945 Government. He and three other MPs were going to Italy to present a Speaker's Chair to the newly formed and only recently democratically elected Parliament. For some reason Ivor had come to our house the day before departing on his mission. During the course of conversation with Anne and Susan he mentioned that the next day he was going to Italy.

"That's the country where the apple trees fruit twice a year", said Anne.

"What's that?" asked Ivor.

"Oh! Didn't you know?" replied Anne. "In Central Italy there are some areas where the climate is so good and the ground so fertile that apple trees fruit there twice a year."

The next day Ivor and his colleagues were speeding by train through France on the way to Italy. Conversation was desultory. None of the four had ever been to Italy; none spoke the language and no-one

---

[60] *More on Tom Driberg at the end of this chapter*

[61] Parents' National Educational Union

appeared to have looked at a guidebook. Thus do some of our representatives prepare for important diplomatic missions.

"I heard an interesting fact about Italy only yesterday", said Ivor. "In some parts apple trees fruit twice in a year".

"That's interesting", said one of the party. "Who told you this?"

"A very eminent authority on Italy with whom I was having a discussion".

On the strength of the fact that he had consulted an authority he was unanimously elected leader of the mission by the others. When he came back to England, the mission was regarded as so successful that he was promoted. He never mentioned that his 'eminent authority' was under six years old.

* * *

My first contact with Tom Driberg was in the run-up to my by-election victory in Chelmsford in April 1945. I knew nothing of him except that he was the Independent Member for Maldon, the neighbouring Essex Parliamentary constituency, and that he was a well-known journalist. He had a deep-seated anti-Establishment attitude to social and political matters and, unsolicited by me, he used his columns in various newspapers and magazines – he was early on befriended by Lord Beaverbrook – to support my candidature. I remember him asking me in an interview about my attitude to Munich (meaning the Munich conference, which was set up to resolve the Allied governments' policy for the future of Germany). My ironic reply was, "I bombed it three times", which Tom took as a subtle rejection of the political decisions made at the conference. So for my by-election I had two influential journalistic allies, the Daily Mirror and Tom Driberg. I was duly elected and met him again as a fellow M.P. in the House of Commons. Because we were both independent of the great political parties we were able to go to one another's constituencies and give political support.

I knew very soon that Tom was homosexual. Enough people wanted to warn me, but I took the liberal view that his sexuality was his own business. From time to time at the conclusion of the day's business in the House of Commons, and when he had clearly had a few large whiskies throughout the evening, he would ask me if I would see him safely home to his flat. I realise now that he was fearful of wandering abroad about the clubs and back streets of Soho and being arrested for some illegal, or at least improper, behaviour. He always paid for his taxi to take me on to Liverpool Street from which I took a train home to Chelmsford. He had in his flat, as I remember, a slender Italian youth as housekeeper: knowing Tom was homosexual I dismissed the young man as a live-in lover. That was his business and that of the boy. And so it progressed for the five years before I lost my seat in Parliament. I had little occasion for contact with him. Perhaps the fact that I was a 16 stone former pilot, former rugby footballer, heterosexual father of four would account for the fact that once the political tie was broken there was nothing to keep us as friends. I only knew of him what I read of his writings in the Press. He had no occasion to know more about me.

Gwen, however, sought to change all that. In 1949 she gave birth to our fourth daughter, Caroline. Gwen always had an eye for the social occasion. The christening of her youngest daughter was to be such an occasion on a grand scale. The Bishop of Chelmsford was to conduct the service. The godparents were a Miss Cecily Pelly, whose brother was a Canon of the Church of England, and Tom Driberg M.P. It was at about this time that I discovered that Tom was a member of the Church of England Finance Committee, and highly regarded in those church circles where he was not personally known. The day came and we foregathered for the christening at Boreham Church. One of the godparents was missing. Tom Driberg had sent along a deputy to act for him. By now the vicar of Kelveden, a neighbouring village, the man who made the vows on Tom's behalf was the man who, as Conservative candidate, had been defeated by him in the General Election.

We saw very little of Tom Driberg from then on. I did not move in any of the circles in which he moved. I think he was the beneficiary of the convention in the Press that dog does not eat dog. Certainly neither my wife nor I had heard any scandal. Perhaps we read the wrong newspapers. The Times and the Observer were even less gossip journals in those days than they are today. It was therefore a shock when, as one does when one is given a book of reference, I ruffled through the pages of a newly acquired Brewer's *Rogues, Villains, Eccentricities,* looking to see if anybody I knew or had known was included.

I came to the entry *Driberg, Tom (1905-76)* and was amazed to read: '... politician and predatory homosexual, befriended by Lord Beaverbrook and by the East End gangster Ronnie Kray, whose homosexual orgies Driberg attended, sometimes in the company of Lord Boothby...'

I had nothing to gain and much to lose in self-respect by allowing myself contact with groups that entertained themselves with homosexual orgies. I sought no further contact with Tom.

Tom died at the age of 71. He was a man of great talents. It was a dreadful shame that the needs of his lower self prevailed and left him basically unfulfilled. He had started as a young graduate praised by Edith Sitwell as 'one of the young poets of the future'; he had been professionally adopted by Lord Beaverbrook; he was a great columnist in more than one journal; yet his life must have been a torment to live. His was a sad failure.[62]

* * *

It would need to be a very ambitious and determined young politician who could sit on the benches of the House of Commons for hours and days on end and pretend to enjoy it. I was a reluctant and totally unambitious M.P. In my case, as the sole member of a political party which was of no significance in the House or in the country, ambition would have been a very false god for me to have worshipped. Furthermore, the basic theme of my political philosophy was one which, whenever I gave voice to any part of it, was profoundly unpopular.

I held, and do even more so at the age of eighty-nine, that more than the ties of religion the enlarged tribal feeling of membership of the nation of one's birth has been in all modern history the cause of hatred and jealousy leading to bloodshed, murder and war. When World War Two broke out the two most significant events in world affairs were the magnificent heroism of the governments and the young people of what once constituted the British Empire in volunteering to come to the aid of the 'Mother Country', and – in marked contrast – the determination of the American Government to get every possible advantage from the world situation. This attitude was not shared by all Americans. A

---

[62] *Tom Driberg was educated at Lancing College – he joined the Communist Party at 15. In 1928 he joined the Daily Express as a gossip columnist and Beaverbrook soon gave him his own column: he used the pen name William Hickey. At the beginning of the War he was recruited into MI5 (and expelled from the Communist Party when Anthony Blunt informed Harry Pollitt that this was the case). He became an independent M.P. in 1942, and stayed in Parliament until 1974, having been a member of the N.E.C. and its chairman in 1957-8. His autobiography Ruling Passions was published after his death in 1976: in it he provided details about his sexual activities (which for much of his life were illegal) and made the term cottaging (picking up homosexual partners in public lavatories) a more widely known term. CM*

significant number of young Americans volunteered for service in the Canadian services and were only reclaimed by America when, two years later, it entered the war. The Americans who had opted to serve in the Allied cause and who had joined the Canadian Air Force were, when they were claimed back by the U.S. Air Force, allowed to complete their tour of operations with the Canadians, wearing Canadian blue uniforms but sporting at the top of their left sleeves the small letters 'U.S.A.' I was outside the George Hotel late one evening talking amongst others to an American officer who was completing a tour of duty with the Canadians. He was waiting for a taxi. Others came along and it was his turn. As he went to take his place in the cab he was quite violently pushed aside by a corporal in the uniform of the American Air Force.

"I can give you twice what he can", shouted the corporal.

"Oh no you can't", said the officer, revealing his shoulder badge. "Go to the back of the queue and wait your turn or I will call the M.P.[63] over there" – who happened to be an American Red Cap – "and have you arrested as a disgrace to American servicemen." The corporal disappeared.

Sometimes on my birthday, but more frequently at Christmas, I hear from New Zealanders like my great friend Mervyn Croker and my equally constant Australian friend McCullough, who came to England as soon as war was declared and volunteered for flying duties immediately. All aircrew, like all submariners and all members of the S.A.S.[64], are volunteers. I cannot refrain from emphasising that these young men were *double* volunteers. They offered themselves as fighting men on Britain's behalf and they volunteered for what proved to be one of the most dangerous of wartime activities, operational flying. Whatever my changed circumstances were during my wartime flying career, I always had at least one or two colleagues from the Dominions. They were all stalwart, brave and utterly dependable. Sadly, they did not all survive.

* * *

I did not enjoy being a Member of Parliament. The hours away from home, wife and children were interminable. Income was nugatory, expenditure high. Everyone came with a problem for the M.P. to solve.

---

[63] M.P. – Military Policeman
[64] S.A.S. – Special Air Service

Some were even satisfied. One wonders whether a young man with little to offer in the way of expertise and experience other than in killing and devastation could achieve anything of sufficient value to justify such a neglect of family. I was not displeased when my constituents came to their senses in 1950 and returned to their traditional Tories for representation.

I returned to the labour market. Still poor, still unable to satisfy all the needs of my family. Able to help people solve their problems. Many other people – but not me. I was glad to leave Parliament in 1950, and start the struggle once again to make a living in some more mundane way to support my family.

13

I suppose I am either too proud or too stupid to cash in on acquaintance or friendship with men in positions of power and influence to achieve something for myself. I used to keep files of copies of letters of introduction which I had written for others. Sometimes for constituents whom I had not even met. Sometimes for servicemen who had an injustice to be investigated. Sometimes for servicemen of my acquaintance who wanted an introduction which was a little more influential than a simple reference. I hardly ever turned any request away, though I was careful not to be fulsome on behalf of total strangers.

I learnt that lesson early. One day I received a green card – an application from a visitor to speak privately to an M.P. In the Central Lobby I met the slight figure of a twenty year old, dressed in mufti. He told me that he was being invalided out of the R.A.F. in which he had been a Sergeant air-gunner. He had been interviewed by a representative of the Ministry of Labour and offered training – as a steeplejack. Unfortunately he was being discharged on the grounds that he was suffering from Meniere's Disease.[65] By coincidence, I was dining that evening with a doctor friend. He produced for me a matchbox.

"Imagine", he said, "that your inner ear conforms approximately to the shape of a matchbox standing on one side. From the upper part there hang vertically about a million tiny hairs. From each side there protrude a similar number which project horizontally. Each hair is sensitively connected with the part of the brain which controls balance. The vertical ones trigger off an automatic reaction to correct a tendency to fall either forward or backwards. The horizontal hairs instruct immediate correction if you are falling sideways."

Clearly for a young person suffering from Meniere's Disease, the trade of steeple-jack was the last thing that he should follow. So I went into action. I arranged for him to be interviewed collectively by Ness

---

[65] *Meniere's Disease is a disease of the inner ear. Its main symptom is vertigo.*

Edwards, Under Secretary of State at the Ministry of Labour and Geoffrey de Freitas, who had a similar job at the Air Ministry. At the due time the next morning the two young ministers and I met at an appointed place. There was a fourth member present who Geoffrey de Freitas introduced simply by name.

"I am an officer of the Fraud Squad at Scotland Yard", he said. "We hope very much that this young man will turn up to this meeting. He is not an R.A.F. Sergeant. He is not being medically discharged. He has not got Meniere's Disease. He is in fact an Army deserter of the former rank of Corporal. He has produced this convincing tear-jerker of a story and he goes round to people who he thinks have a few bob and will tip him a fiver or a tenner. The last thing he wants is any kind of official contact or investigation".

I am bound to say that if I had not been keen to try out the new government's approach to the alleviation of individual hardship, and had had a fiver to spare - what a hope – I might have fallen for his scam.

However, to revert to my opening thought. My life has comprised alternative periods which can only be described as 'highs', followed by more sustained weeks, and sometimes months, of 'lows'. When I was demobilised from the R.A.F. I had just been elected to the House of Commons. Although one did not, in those days, enter the House in order to make one's fortune, there was attached to the rank and status a reasonable salary. Until I was demobilised (the countdown for which did not start until the war against Japan was over) I was in receipt – in addition to my Parliamentary pay – of pay as a Wing Commander. I was well off, at least by my standards. A few months after I was elected to Parliament my Wing Commander pay stopped. And in 1950 I lost my Parliamentary pay as well. Instead of a reasonable joint income which made for middle class comfort I was left with nothing, except the comparatively tiny unemployment pay. The dole is not only the name of the small allowance made to the unemployed, it also – very appropriately – has another meaning: 'dolour' or extreme sadness.

By this time I had four dependent children and a wife who let me know that a husband's duty was to provide for his family in the manner the wife thought appropriate. There were one or two agencies which claimed to find employment for odd-bods who fitted with no specific category. I applied. Sometimes I was called for interview. It seemed to me that nobody wanted to say that the market was not open for men with no qualifications except for dropping bombs and with a political background that was not comforting to aspiring capitalists. So I became familiar with such phrases as *over-qualified, lacking in commercial experience* or even just plain *who wants to employ an under-educated young man with an anti-capitalist background?*

I realise now that there were many jobs which fell under the control of members of the 1945 Labour Government – Ministers or their appointed successors – for which I might have made application. My former W.E.A. Economics tutor, Dr Monica Felton, who had given me much encouragement when I was a young W.E.A. student, was now chairman of the managers of a New Town. I realise that others who had lost their Parliamentary seats in 1950 applied for and were given opportunities of which I might have availed myself. I look back and wonder whether the fact that I failed to get in touch with Monica or with the Minister of Health, who was in charge of the initial appointments in the development of the new towns (my old friend Aneurin Bevan), was because of modesty, stupidity or idleness. Whatever the reason, I did not take up any such contact.

It must be a sign of a truly optimistic spirit that it is hard to recall periods of very low fortune. Undoubtedly with the children needing maintenance in the holidays – Anne, Susan and Deborah had scholarship support to go to boarding school in term time – it must have been extremely hard on Gwen. Anne and Susan were both at Christ's Hospital in Hertford and Deborah, who had delighted us all from a very early age with her elfin dancing, had gone to the Arts Educational School at Tring.

There came a bit of nonsense of which I am not a little ashamed. Whilst I was still a sitting Member of Parliament I had allowed myself to be persuaded to organise a visit to Denmark of the band of the Office Training Corps of Chelmsford Grammar School. Raising money was extremely difficult and apart from the Headmaster of the school, who seemed to me to come as of right, the applications from free-loaders to come 'to help with the administration' were numerous. In the end we settled for the band master, a Captain Lewis, and friends of his whose names I have forgotten – a married couple. Lewis and his friends went out with the band by sea. Clearly bulky instruments could not easily – or cheaply – go by air. The Headmaster and I flew out, planning to arrive in time to greet the boys. As one does on journeys, we found ourselves chatting to a very formally dressed civilian who explained that he was in charge at the Foreign Office of putting forward the names of serving officers for duty as Army, Navy or Air Force Attaches at British Embassies throughout the capital cities of the world. What a pity I was not a serving officer, he said. With a background of politics I would certainly be of greater value to the Government than the usual appointees who were better known for the smartness of their uniforms than for the sharpness of their brains. Had I ever thought of going back into the R.A.F? If I ever did so I was to get in touch and he would put my name forward for interview with a view to appointment as Air Attaché. He gave me a card with his name and an extension in the Air Ministry. I must say it looked like one of my serendipitous meetings.

After the 1950 Election when I was not returned to Parliament, there was a period of earning in bits and pieces. So, after discussion with Gwen, I applied to rejoin the R.A.F. Sadly I was by now considered too old to go back to flying. I was offered a commission two ranks below Wing Commander in the administrative branch. We were going through a very lean time, and both agreed that I should accept. So I became a non-flying Flight Lieutenant in the R.A.F. Pay, of course, was without the addition of flying pay and considerably less than I had received as a Wing Commander, but we managed. I qualified, as a married officer, for quarters at a very reasonable rent and we settled into our new way of life. By 1952 I was Personal Assistant to the Commandant of R.A.F. Halton in Buckinghamshire. He was Air Commodore Tindal-Caryl-Worsley, and we got on very well. Even more important, Gwen got on well with Mrs T-C-W, and Halton was not too far from Hertford, for visiting Anne and Susan, or Tring for visiting Deborah. I stayed for several years at Halton.

They had a well-run Amateur Dramatic Society run by an officer of the Education department. I featured as the Commander-in-Chief of the French Army, as a drunken lay-about and as an almost senile suitor – not, of course, all in the same play. Gwen became an official in the wives' club. We enjoyed a full and enjoyable, though very poverty-stricken, life.

Then, in 1956, came the Suez crisis. The British Government threatened to take over the Suez Canal by force, although it was due to come under international jurisdiction within a couple of years. Threats were made by the government, which sought to justify itself on the grounds that national self-interest required us to safeguard the shorter route from Europe to India which, it was claimed, was under threat. We had no allies. France and Germany took us to the United Nations. America threatened to intervene. The Conservative Government of Sir Anthony Eden was obdurate.

In the midst of this sabre-rattling we were ordered to convene two parades, one of all the airmen and N.C.O.s who could be spared from essential duties, and the other of all the officers. The two meetings were to hear a Government spokesman who was touring military establishments to explain the precise political position and its possible military consequences. Partly because I am a very nosy fellow, and partly because it seemed the only courteous thing to do, I attended the Other Ranks meeting. I was the only officer present.

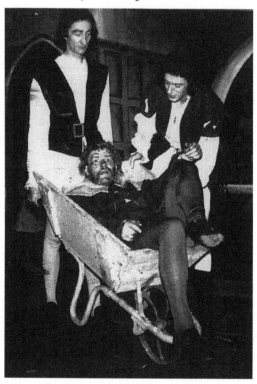

'The Lady's Not For Burning' – R.A.F. Halton Amateur Dramatics 1954

The representative of the Government turned out to be a rabid rightwing Hungarian academic who harangued the troops about the Red Menace, and how it behoved every loyal and patriotic Englishman to be prepared to fight for our country's right to the Freedom of the Seas. We then went in the afternoon of the same day to the Officers' meeting. There I heard an entirely different speech from the same man. None of the near-hysterical appeal to patriotic emotions. Rather a reasonable and reasoned analysis of a crisis which, at that moment, was being argued out and would be resolved diplomatically. One must remember that I was the only officer who had heard both speeches. I protested that when he had made two different appeals he had been, at the very least, insulting to the intelligence of the airman audience. There was nothing to confirm what I said. The other officers had only heard the second, reasoned speech. They thought I was exaggerating, if not making it up. That my criticism were racist because the officer was Hungarian. And so on.

Prime Minister Anthony Eden flying out of R.A.F. Halton (Copyright © "The Bucks Herald")

The Commandant sent for me and told me that he felt compelled to report the incident to Group Headquarters. A few days later I was sent for by the Group Captain, Admin., who had with him a civilian who, he said, was a senior officer from the Security Services. He discussed the enormity of what I had done and, as I was dismissed, assured me that I would live to regret it. Soon after, I was posted to Malta.

* * *

In the run up to my removal to Malta, I was aware that I was under considerable pressure. New and arduous duties were thrust upon me, terminating in my last evening. I was being dined out, guest of honour at a formal Mess dinner at which it clearly became the duty of everyone present to ply me with as much alcohol as possible. At round about midnight apparently I was called to the door of the Mess and a Sergeant handed me the proceeds of an airman's dance, which had just finished. I put the envelope unopened in my pocket. It contained the sum of 28s 6d.[66] I have no recollection of this occurrence. I had been well and truly dined out. The next day I left for Malta.

Gwen and Caro had already left. Anne, Susan and Deborah had gone off to stay with Auntie Vera at Southend. My preoccupation with all my duties had not left time for me to obtain clearance from all the departments with which I had had business over the past few weeks. This included a civilian clerk who was responsible for the accounts of the Wives' Club, of which my wife had been treasurer. I had been given responsibility for the R.A.F. side of the Wives' Club. They used R.A.F. premises. Their accounts were administered by the civilian clerk. I did not get 'clearance' from this clerk under pressure of time and other duties. Some months after my arrival in Malta I was interviewed by a Wing Commander of the R.A.F. police. I was accused of stealing 28s 6d, which had been handed to me on my dining out night and that, in conspiracy with my wife, I had stolen about £50 which had been drawn by the Wives' Club and not accounted for. I was flown back from Malta, leaving my wife and daughter there.

The investigating officer said that he had been in touch with the Chief Constable of Essex and that a move was afoot to bring Gwen and Caroline back to England; Gwen to answer a joint charge of theft. She would have to be tried in a civil court. On being pressed by me he admitted that he had not yet got in touch with the civilian police. He would not press this step if I confessed to the theft charges. I realised that the 28s 6d was a clear case of oversight and would be repaid immediately, although I had no recollection of the incident which was alleged to have taken place when I was probably too drunk to remember. Furthermore I asked permission to visit my civilian bank, which was ten miles from the camp. It would be difficult, as I would have to persuade my bank manager to grant me a small unsecured loan, so that I could put the sum of money in question in the station adjutant's safe as admission of my ability to pay if evidence of ability to pay was sought. The R.A.F. policeman said that he could not permit that as I was under arrest. He would not, however, pursue any approach to the civilian police in respect of Gwen if I confessed.

I was torn. I had no desire to confess to a crime that I had not committed. On the other hand, he put great pressure on me by arguing

---

[66] *Equivalent to one pound and 42 pence*

that only a confession would prevent him from having Gwen (with Caroline) brought back from Malta to be charged with conspiracy to rob. Rather than have my wife involved in what was clearly a vendetta against me, I entered into a compromise agreement that he would not involve Gwen but could go ahead with pressing charges against me. Had anything like that happened to me now, I would take a publish-and-be-damned attitude, but I was younger and anxious to protect my family. I now realise that there was no intention to call in the civil police, who would have refused to take action on such flimsy evidence.

The long, slow process of investigation was set in motion. I was not allowed to return to Malta. My financial position was thoroughly investigated. It revealed that I was struggling on the margin. A court of inquiry was set up in which a Squadron Leader was appointed to interview me, which he did with great frequency, and to take evidence of character from a multiplicity of witnesses, none of whom I was asked to nominate. Eventually the papers went to the Commander in Chief. I sincerely believe he was under orders to ensure that I was discharged from the R.A.F. by hook or by crook. I was remanded for Court Martial on two charges: not fulfilling all the requirements demanded by regulations of the officer posted abroad, and theft of 28s 6d and an undetermined sum of around £50. Not unnaturally the story got – was leaked? – to the Press. 'Ex left-wing M.P. charged with fraud'. 'Wartime hero, peacetime crook?'

The very worst thing that happened to me was that I received a visit from a former Chelmsford solicitor who had moved to Aylesbury. His name was Wyc (possibly a contraction of Wycliffe) Hill. He was ambitious to become accepted as a 'solicitor advocate', which would entitle him to plead on the same terms as a barrister in courts higher than a magistrate's court. He offered, nay insisted, to be allowed to act for me when my court martial was convened, For old times' sake he would be glad to appear without charging any fee. I was in such a state that I felt I had to agree. Any friends I thought I had had deserted. Not quite true. Somebody from the House of Commons remembered me. In any case they thought that the charge would at most fetch a remand in a civil court. I received letters of support and cheques, most of them for £25, from several of my former colleagues.

The date set arrived. The court opened. It consisted of three senior R.A.F. officers with a civilian lawyer from the Judge Advocate General's department to advise. The charges were read and the prosecution called its witnesses. Wyc Hill was appalling. He was totally ignorant of Court Martial procedure and had continually to be corrected and told to sit down. He did not listen to any suggestions I made, especially when he was cross examining prosecution witnesses. In his final address in my defence he did not apply himself to the charges, but gave an irrelevant and histrionic speech about what a good M.P. I had been when he had known me in Chelmsford. It was clearly all in vain. I was found guilty and ordered to be cashiered from the R.A.F.

* * *

You will no doubt recall that the whole of this incident arose from the Suez crisis of 1956. Nearly two years had passed, and I was now a disgraced ex-R.A.F. officer with a wife and youngest daughter in Malta, my oldest daughter at Oxford University and the two middle daughters in Southend with Vera Smith. I had no home, no money, the suit I stood up in and little to look forward to. I say no money, because I had sent the bulk of the money I had received from former MP colleagues to Gwen in Malta. I had received a great deal of supportive mail from well-wishers who thought the whole process of arrest and court martial and particularly the verdict and sentence were profoundly unjust. Amongst them was one from Alec McCullough, a former R.A.F. lieutenant and now the landlord of a public house near Mount Pleasant, the main G.P.O. sorting office in London, which was called the Exmouth Arms. He did not beat about the bush, but said that I was welcome to come and stay at his pub, with or without members of my family, if I were stuck. I took him at this word.

As I approached the Exmouth Arms I saw there was an ambulance outside. Being carried out on a stretcher was a man whom I correctly guessed to be McCullough. I went to him, introduced myself and asked if there was anything I could do.

"Look after Phil", he said, "She is pregnant. Tell her I want you to manage the pub for me. I don't trust all the staff. Stay as long as you like."

Instead of being homeless, at least I had regular food and drink and somewhere to lay my head. I was now managing a tough pub with a regular clientele of postal workers and a fair number of local lay-abouts, many of whom came in for warmth.[67] They often arrived fairly sozzled

---

[67] *Exmouth Market is now the centre of desirable and expensive restaurants and shops. This was not the case in the 1950s.*

on methylated spirits which were much stronger than beer or cider. Typical of the clients was an old lady, ragged of clothing and ruddy of face, who was always half seas over. One evening, overwhelmed by the weight of liquor in her bladder, she had upped with her skirt and down with her drawers and was caught peeing in the gutter by the evening police patrol. It was a widely held local rumour, totally untrue, that the acting manager of the pub had shopped her to the police and was responsible for her arrest. She was charged with indecent exposure and found guilty. She, at least, never returned to the Exmouth Arms.

After a few days I received unexpected relief. Mrs McCullough had sent for her brother in Ireland. I am a six-footer. He towered over me. His name was Vincent. On the day of his arrival he settled into a room in the pub and found himself a bookmaker. All before lunch. After making his number with me, I heard him making a complicated bet on the telephone. It was a £1 win treble: that is a £1 bet to win was placed against a horse. If it won, the stake money and winnings were placed on a second horse. If that horse won, the whole of the money won was to be placed on a third horse to win. He told me that there were three good horses from Ireland that had never run before in England. Would I like a piece of the action? More than anything to establish good relations with somebody who was going to work with me, I agreed and handed over a ten shilling note for a half share in his bet. Late that afternoon I was in the bar preparing for the evening session. He came in looking very crestfallen.

"So we've lost our money", I said. "Bad luck".

"Not at all – we won! I'm sad because I owe you half!"

He took out of his pocket a bundle of notes and gave me, I seem to remember, about £35. He turned out to be just the kind of barman I needed. There was a lot of drunkenness and occasional unrestrained violence. Vincent kept a baseball bat behind the bar. Not for him my technique which was to try to get between any warring factions. Vincent would leap over the bar, clutching his baseball bat. A few dextrously placed taps would render the combatants semi – or temporarily – unconscious.

"Ring up the police and tell them to send round a van to pick up the two drunks we have had to put out for fighting".

He would then drag them outside and lean them against the wall to await the law. Meanwhile Gwen and Caroline were on their way back to England from Malta.

14

Gwen and Caroline joined me at the Exmouth Arms. We did not stay long. McCullough returned, glad enough of the happy accident which had brought the homeless to his door just as he was leaving for hospital. Gwen's suburban convent school upbringing and rather spoilt life as an officer's wife – and later as a C.O.'s wife – had not fitted her for the outrageous sordidness of life in a pub in a very poor district of central London. When the landlord came back he showed a remarkable eccentricity of character. He liked to clean and play with a revolver. I knew that it was never loaded and therefore no more dangerous than any other piece of inert metal. But to the more gently reared Gwen the sight of a man regularly handling such a dangerous-looking mechanism was, to say the least of it, very unnerving. He also had the very noisy habit of working amongst the full and empty barrels in the cellar long after Gwen and Caroline's bedtime. So we told him that we would be moving on.

He wished us well and thrust a small bundle of bank-notes into my hand. Apparently all pub-managers manipulate their finances so as to leave a regular flow of cash which neither finds their bank account nor the accounts of the Inland Revenue. He was genuinely glad to see us go just as we had been glad of his initial generous offer of hospitality and now strongly felt the need to find somewhere else to live. Caroline had by this time reached primary school age. She was attending Sir Christopher Hatton Primary School which seems to have been the most successful part of life in Clerkenwell. We had therefore to find somewhere from which she could continue to go to the same school. Since we had no home and no furniture a Bed and Breakfast establishment seemed the only possibility.

The one we found was a large house owned and run as a business by a married couple in Finsbury Park. Mr Dalrymple was a very black man of Caribbean origin. He was courteous and gentle sounding although I never saw him doing a stroke of work more strenuous than collecting the rent. His wife was blonder than what usually passes for blondness. Her hair was white, but in no way the white of advanced years. I felt that she was the dynamo that ran the business. We were interviewed in their sitting room. It was a great shock to us both. It was lavish in its ornamentation and decoration. The rooms for rent were more sparsely fitted out. As soon as we had moved in I set about two urgent tasks. The first was to find a home of our own, and the other to find employment.

We found a house in Islington – number 6, Battledean Road – which suited us admirably. It was a tall, thin three-storey house which had clearly been let off as three flats as there was a gas meter in cupboards on all three floors. The meters had been disconnected and each showed a reading of *NIL GAS* consumed. It was, therefore, a shock to receive an invoice for each meter demanding immediate payment of £0.0s.0d.[68] Non-payment would inevitably be followed by disconnection. I ignored the demand, which was followed up by another, ending with an even stronger threat, for £0.0s.0d. So I sent off a cheque for this precise amount with a request that the disconnected meters should be removed. I received a receipt for my cheque and a man called to collect the meters. If this isn't the strangest story of bureaucracy in action, I would like to know what is.

The house was the property of Islington Borough Council. I had heard somewhere that Islington was very helpful to first-time buyers with very little money. I was entrusted with the keys. Having no reply to my enquiry about aided purchase of the council house, we moved in. It was six months before I received a reply accepting me as a suitable purchaser, suggesting a very cheap purchase price – I seem to remember a figure of £5,500 – and asking for a small deposit. I thought it a very generous offer from the Council, especially as we had been living rent-free for six months. So I signed the paper and paid the deposit.

One of my problems was resolved. I had found a house. Somewhere along the line I had been permitted to store my furniture in the very large house at the gates of Wormwood Scrubs prison where the Rev. Charles Watts, who had for years been a good friend and political supporter, was the current chaplain. He was the occupant of a large house just outside the gates of the prison. We had been delighted to accept his kind offer to accommodate our furniture and thus had it readily available when we wanted to move into 6 Battledean Road.

---

[68] *Pre-decimalisation of sterling – no pounds, no shillings and no pence.*

My next urgent task was to find a job which would provide an income for a wife and family. It never occurred to me to contact any of my former colleagues from the House of Commons, some of whom had important jobs in post-war reconstruction. Pride? Laziness? Stupidity? I just didn't think of trying to cash in on old contacts. Instead I looked at Situations Vacant columns in the newspapers. Everybody wanted University graduates. But wait. What is this?

American servicemen and their families in England are starved for education. Why not join the growing number of men and women who are making a good living, after training, by meeting this need?

I telephoned and went for an interview. First one was taught a patter which, it was claimed, opened many a front door with an invitation to go within. What one had to sell was a small number of beautifully bound source books – History, Geography, Relations between States etc. The piece de resistance, however, was a set of twenty encyclopaedias in which, it was claimed, the student could find an answer to any academic question. Actually they weren't as good as all that, but it was not a stain on one's conscience to try to persuade a young American serviceman, with a wife and small family, to invest in them.

The commission was good and, apart from the tendency which I had to enter into friendly conversation, all went reasonably well. I managed to sell enough to eke out a not unreasonable income. At least we had enough to pay the mortgage and to eat comfortably. But not enough to enjoy the luxury of car ownership. The Americans lived mainly in the neighbourhood of Harrow. We were in Islington. I could get to my daily destination quite comfortably by bus, but my income varied dramatically according to the amount of commission I received from week to week. Some weeks I did well. Rejoicings in the Millington household. Some weeks I received almost nothing, a percentage of what I had sold. Consequence: until I started to make money I walked from Islington to Harrow, did my day's calling and walked back.

One day I had been driven off the doorstep by torrential rain. I trudged drearily back towards home. As I turned into Gray's Inn Road, just by King's Cross Station, I noticed something white standing out in the slush of the day. I went across and picked up an immaculate piece of paper which clearly must have been dropped only a minute or two previously. It was an open company cheque for something over £375, and endorsed 'Please Pay Bearer'. We were standing outside the bank on which the cheque was drawn. The office of the company to which the cheque belonged was immediately opposite. It would be untruthful for me to say that I wasn't tempted; the cheque was for an amount which would have kept my family in comparative luxury for over a month. The cheque was endorsed Pay to Bearer and I was outside the bank. I may not have made a purely ethical decision. I may have been thinking of the consequences if the bank teller rang the company and asked for verification of my right to draw money on their behalf. Whatever my motive, I found myself at the reception desk of the company concerned.

There was no-one in reception. Along a corridor leading from it I could see into two offices. People were searching everywhere. Waste paper baskets were emptied on tables and the contents were being meticulously sorted. There was a bell on the receptionist's desk. I ran it vigorously. Nobody came. I took the cheque out of my pocket, unfolded it and held it up in the air between my fingers. Still nobody came. Eventually a young man came out of one of the offices, saw me and what I was holding. He ran up and snatched the cheque then rushed off into the office, calling out the glad news that that which was lost had been found. All the people who had been searching departed into the office with the young man. I waited for someone to come out and thank me. I waited five minutes. Ten minutes. A quarter of an hour. It became clear that nobody was going to acknowledge their saviour. So I left and trudged wearily down to Islington.

The company concerned was called Lesney: they made small toys that fitted into matchboxes. I never again bought a small toy that fitted into a matchbox.

* * *

As so often occurs in my life when I am at an all-time low, a casual remark of an acquaintance gives me the inspiration to try a new tack. "There is a shortage of teachers", was the remark that set it off. Although I had attained the grade of Above Average as a flying instructor, I knew enough about the theory of training in a skill, as opposed to education – helping to develop the whole person – to realise that I could not really make a request for my experience as a flying instructor to transfer to the education of children. Quite frankly, I was facing the rare predicament of feeling that I was not good enough. Now that I have had many years' experience of teachers I know that the feeling was based on a false judgement. 'Those who can, do; those who can't, teach.'

I was conscious of the fact that my academic qualifications were limited to three Higher Schools certificates which, being in Greek, Latin and French, rather limited the kind of schools which could use my basic training. In any case I had taken these certificate examinations at the age of sixteen and had no formal education since, apart from learning to fly and drop bombs. However, I wrote to the College of St Mark and St John, which in those days was in Kensington, on the route of the number 19 bus which ran virtually past where I was living in Islington.

I was summoned for interview. The panel consisted of the Principal and Vice Principal of the College. In those days one did not include a curriculum vitae. One wrote a self-advancing letter to accompany the application form. In it, I referred to the fact that I had had a recent review published in the New Statesman. This made a stronger impression than any question of rank or experience. Both my interviewers had failed, after repeated attempts, to get something published in the New Statesman. I had the advantage (which I did not mention) of being personally friendly with John Freeman, who had just taken over as Editor. My interview must have broken all speed records. They wanted to know nothing about my career in the R.A.F., nothing about my qualifications as a flying instructor. Only a few brief questions about getting something published in the New Statesman. All my misgivings were swept away. I was accepted for training without demur.

In those days teacher training was a two year course. Exceptionally one could join a high speed one year course. To my astonishment I was accepted for the shortened course. Not all the staff were happy to have the high speed course running. I can remember the head of the English department, one Sid Heaven. He was a Plaistow boy who had played water polo for England. On the basis of his athletic and sporting skills he had been accepted for the teacher training course. I was full of admiration for his determination and the fact that he had, on merit, worked his way up to become Head of Department. He did not like me. I was a public schoolboy. I had had a not undistinguished career in the R.A.F. I had been a Member of Parliament, I was a mature student accepted for a shortened course. I apologise if I am wrong, but it seemed to me then – and still does – a clear case of inverted snobbery.

Other members of the staff I remember with affection. One had been a Professor of Philosophy in an Eastern Europe university. When Czechoslovakia adopted communism he, and other foreign academics, were banned from their jobs and eventually ordered out of the country. So he came to England. A highly qualified and experienced fifty year old.

Anathema to the Establishment which loves the principle of Buggin's Turn. He taught English beautifully, and to another over-age entrant to the profession he could not have been more helpful.

Towards the end of my year I had completed his course on the History of Education, various schools of Education and a smattering of quasi-philosophy of Education. In the autumn term there came an anguished request from the local Education Authority. Was there a student sufficiently advanced to take over a class for the month before Christmas during the class teacher's maternity leave? The course I was on was for Secondary School teachers, so it was a bit of a shock to discover that the class referred to were top infants – seven year olds.

My Course Principal knew that I had four children, which was more than could be said with assurance for the 19-21 year olds who made up the rest of the course. He also knew I would be paid – admittedly as an unqualified teacher – and that that would be more than the student allowance on which we had been struggling to exist. So I went to take over a class of thirty or so seven year olds for a month. The school was two teachers under strength, even after my arrival. The headmistress had no time to guide or train me, as she had a full time teaching load. There was such a shortage of infant teachers that there were no supply teachers available. I thus became that rare phenomenon in an infant school, a 43 year old man, with no infant training, with a class of thirty infants and nobody to give me advice or assistance.

"Do what you like with them, so long as it keeps them quiet and doesn't cost too much money".

When I met my class they were restless and amazed to have a male teacher. I started off by asking them what was coming in about a month's time. After some prodding, for they were a strange mixture of shyness and aggression, they recognised that we were only four weeks away from Christmas.

"What do you like most about Christmas?" I asked.

"Presents," was the favourite reply, closely followed by "Food".

"What's your favourite food at Christmas?"

We went through a complete Christmas Day menu which revealed a wide diversity between the expectations of the well-to-do and the very poor. Not for the very poor the turkey, mince-pies and other delicacies which were taken for granted by the more affluent. However there was a consensus. Favourite Christmas fare was Christmas cake.

I had an inspiration. I had been brought up by a very modern mother who insisted on teaching her three sons, as well as her daughters, to cook. Especially at Christmas time we all joined in with the early preparations of Christmas puddings and Christmas cake. It occurred to me that I could incorporate a great deal of valuable teaching of spelling, geography and how various items of food ingredients were prepared and improved. I could tie it all in with a bit of arithmetic, making shopping lists, weighing and measuring. With luck I could hold their interest profitably until the end of term. So we started. I had a recipe book with a good simple recipe for cake. I promised them a party on my last day, in which we would eat the cake we had made. We built up an interesting vocabulary.

> *Flour.* Where did it come from? Where was wheat grown? Are there any other kinds of flour? Do we want to use them in the cake?

> *Sugar.* Where did it come from? What do we mean by a refinery? Do you have any other than white sugar at your house? What names do we have for yellow or brown sugar? Where are Demerara, Barbados etc? Are they hot countries?

> *Cooking Fats. Butter.* Where does it come from? What do we call a farm for cows? *Margarine.* What is the difference between butter and margarine? Is margarine less expensive than butter (find out from your mother)?

I do not record the above as any example of my teaching methods. The sequel to what we had started amazed me and cannot be made clear unless the reader is aware of the method and the content. The first reaction other than by the children took the form of a visit at the close of morning school early in the project. The senior dinner lady apologised for being in such a rush.

"I must go and supervise lunch. We've heard that as an educational project you are going to make a cake for Christmas. May I say that my ladies and I entirely approve of what you're trying to do. We realise that we must not offer to help in any way with the making of the cake, but we would like to bake it in our kitchen. We would also like to offer to ice it for you, if you like."

I was astonished. My experience and received wisdom was that there existed a degree of hostility between kitchen and classroom. I accepted fulsomely, thinking that perhaps it was due to the fact that I was a man in an all-woman environment and that for the children's sake the dinner ladies wanted the project to be successful. The second reaction was at least as unexpected. Normally mothers came to fetch their children after school, waiting for them at the school gate. They began to drift in, asking questions about what I meant to do and offering to help. Then they began to bring in bags of flour, margarine, sugar, eggs and dried fruit until I had to ask them not to bring any more as we had enough ingredients for three or four cakes. More to the point, they offered the loan of mixing bowls, wooden spoons and baking tins.

So we went ahead checking, weighing, working out the prices and gathering as much learning from each step as I could generate. Every child had more than one opportunity to stir the cake mixture – and to lick fingers free of any delicious fragments which were stuck to them. The time came when we packed the cake mixture into two well-greased tins and took them down to the cooks to bake. They did not come back the next day. We all waited with excitement and some trepidation. Eventually, the day before breaking up for Christmas, they came up – beautifully iced and with some Christmas tokens on each one. The words, "A Happy Christmas!", a sprig of holly and a small robin adorned each cake. The next day mothers had been invited for the afternoon session. The cakes were cut up and we all ate pieces. My one and only month as an infant school teacher was over. To me it was a wonderful experience. A great success.

* * *

Early in January I received through the post information that I was a fully accredited teacher and that my certificate would follow. I rang County Hall, headquarters of the London County Council, and was given an appointment with a senior inspector for ten thirty the next morning. At ten thirty I was interviewed. At ten forty five I had a medical examination. At ten fifty five I received a letter introducing me to the headmaster of Pitfield Street Secondary Modern School. At one thirty I was marking the register of my own class there.

15

One has read from time to time of 'sink' schools. It is unlikely that any school can have sunk much lower than Pitfield Street. It was a small eight to ten classroomed nineteenth century building, all on one floor, with a hall that was used for assemblies and as a dining room, and a concrete covered playground. When I arrived the school had just reassembled after the midday break. In the hall were two men. The first, a trim little man of about five foot four, under his arm a book and a cane. He was Mr Arundel, the headmaster. With him was his deputy. Mr Arundel saw me enter the hall and beckoned me over. Suddenly he whirled round and pointed to a boy, visible behind the glass door of a classroon. Mr Arundel indicated that he wanted the boy to come into the hall. Without a word, when he arrived he held out a hand. It received a swingeing whack with the cane. The headmaster indicated the other hand. It received the same treatment. Nothing was said. With a nod of his head the headmaster dismissed the boy to return to his classroom.

"What was that for?" I could not prevent myself asking.

"Nothing in particular. He knows it is for something he thought he had got away with or for some future crime has not yet committed".

He led me to a classroom of about thirty boys.

"This is your class", he said. "This morning's teacher did not stay for school dinner, although he had paid for it".

As soon as the headmaster shut the door behind him and went back into the hall bedlam was let loose. Books and other missiles flew across the room. Everybody seemed to be shouting. Nobody took the slightest notice of me. I saw that one boy had an exercise book on his desk. It had on it his name: Adams, Class 1. Adams was kneeling on his seat facing the boy behind and waving and shouting vehemently. I went up to him and shouted "Adams!" in a loud voice. Barely turning round he exclaimed to me, "You can go and fuck yourself".

Remember, this was my first day of teaching, except for the darling infants I had been with before Christmas. I grabbed his shoulder, wrenched him round so that his stomach was over the desk and his bottom in the air. I smacked it with my strong right hand until I could not have swatted a fly with it. Turning Adams so that he could sit, uncomfortably, at his desk I strode to the teacher's desk. By this time the whole class, which had been in a chaotic state, had assumed their seats and were awaiting events more or less quietly but with an air of some trepidation. Hiding my right hand, which hurt like hell, I growled: "There's plenty more where that came from".

With one exception, I was the only teacher on the staff who had not provided himself with a cane. I did not have occasion to touch a boy in anger for the rest of our stay together.

Although we were a secondary school each teacher was responsible for more than one subject in his own class. As with the unwillingness to possess a cane the one exception to the general rule was the teacher whose specialisation was history. His name was Alan Connolly. He was a sad widower with one child, a ten year old daughter. He taught history by telling stories which he managed to make more alluring than anything the boys saw on television. Every class wanted to have Mr Connolly's weekly history lesson. He could also draw extremely well. So he produced beautifully drawn hand-outs to illustrate what he was going to talk about. These hand-outs were probably the only teaching materials in the school that were looked after with pleasure and respect by the boys.

When Gwen, a few years later, qualified and began work as a primary school teacher, she was fortunate enough to find that Mr Connolly had changed from secondary to primary teaching, which suited his talents and his temperament perfectly, and was on the staff of the first primary school at which she taught. He was lonely and became a great friend to my family.

* * *

Pitfield Street School was scheduled to be closed at the end of term and its staff and pupils to be transferred, with the staff and pupils of Shoreditch Grammar School, to form a new comprehensive school. The headmaster-to-be of the new Shoreditch Comprehensive School was currently the headmaster of the Grammar School. His name was Bussey. The secondary modern element in his new school and their parents terrified him. Whenever a parent arrived the school secretary was instructed to telephone Mr Bussey, who then locked himself in his room, and to send for the deputy headmistress. She was a charming little lady named Mrs Metcalf, who had no difficulty in standing up to an irate docker and his often more irate wife.

I remember one occasion when the deputy head was being harangued by an enormous docker and his wife. What made it worse was that the subject of the controversy, their enormous teenage daughter, was not only there but also insisting on butting in. The one-sided match was in an open space at the foot of a flight of stairs leading to the staff room. The fracas was looking really ugly when a teacher new to the staff, a tough-looking Geordie who had only been with us a couple of weeks, came bounding down the stairs. He grabbed the daughter by the elbow, took her apart and whispered something fiercely in her ear. She immediately stepped back and did not say another word. The discussion cooled down and the animosity diminished. Afterwards I said to him,

"That was marvellous. What did you say to her?"

"Nothing very much", he grinned. "All I said to her was, 'If you don't shut up and hold your fucking tongue I'll hang one on you'."

The last I heard of him he had obtained a Ph.D. and was a senior lecturer at a Teacher Training College. Mr Bussey applied for and obtained the headship of Enfield Grammar School. A year later it was made comprehensive.

* * *

Pitfield Street School had a music teacher who was heartily disliked. At that time Liberace, whose signature was a lighted candelabra on his piano, was in his prime. Every morning at assembly a lit candle was wedged into the neck of a beer bottle, furtively smuggled on to the piano of the music teacher. Nobody was ever caught doing it.

At the end of term we were breaking up for Christmas and would reassemble in the premises of the new Shoreditch Comprehensive School. When I arrived at school on the last day I was confronted by two or three of the bigger boys who were carrying out a mock search.

"What are you looking for?" I asked.

"We're checking up to see if we can spot any teacher who thinks he can buy an easy last day with presents", came the reply.

Just then the music teacher came in carrying several loaded bags. They were taken by the boys. When I left for home the teacher was on the floor behind the piano being pelted with the cakes he had brought in. Because we were a school in the midst of a district which benefited from many charities – University, Catholic, Jewish – there were many gifts, especially of cakes and other edible luxuries, at Christmas time. Somebody had had the sense to bring in a supply of plastic bags, and I observed as I left that most of the boys were filling the bags with goodies to take home to their younger siblings.

* * *

The Shoreditch Comprehensive School into which we all moved was in a new building, populated by the teachers and pupils of the grammar school, Pitfield Street and one other secondary modern. The transfer coincided with the raising of the school leaving age.[69] It was a Devil's Brew. The minority were the rather better adjusted grammar school children. The majority were the sink school secondary modern kids who had expected to leave school at the end of the previous term only to be told that they were legally obliged to stay on for at least one more year. Clearly there was the potential for conflict.

The school was housed in a new building. It was planned to be built in three phases. Phases 1 and 2 were to be ready when the school opened for the first term of its existence. But only Phase 1 was complete. Phase 2 was still a building site. Phase 3 was an overgrown area of rough ground. Not unnaturally the ex-grammar school children, led by the ex-grammar school head teacher, were housed in the Phase 1 buildings. One or two areas in the Phase 2 building were complete and were fitted out as craft rooms; for example, woodwork and needlework. With a bit of squeezing all the ex-grammar school children and the top streams of the secondary moderns could be adequately accommodated in fine new premises. This left one of the old secondary modern buildings, which was due for demolition, and the space used for the new Phase 3 building. In addition there was a large rubbish dump.

Exacerbated by the fact that they were trapped at school by being the ROSLA guinea-pigs, the remainder were left with a derelict school building and an overgrown building site. There were about 150 children, almost all with long records of non-cooperation at previous schools and all furious that they hadn't left to start work – for example, on the market stalls on which they had already been earning evening pocket money sometimes for the previous two or three years. I had one lad whose parents were highly prosperous fruit and veg stall holders. They gave him

---

[69] ROSLA – Raising of the School Leaving Age (from 14 to 16).

his first stall, with certificate to trade and an introduction to wholesalers, for his thirteenth birthday. He was a very useful class member. He could be given a verbal shopping list of fruit and vegetables, with weights and prices per pound, often with the addition of a percentage discount figure for some hypothetical special client. Before the teacher had put down his list the boy had a gross price, discount and net price calculated. He would then write the whole order on the blackboard from memory, without the calculations, and go through each item painstakingly with a select group of the class. He himself made the selection as to who would be in his group. They were mainly his friends and as they became reasonably sound mathematicians they were invited – for a small wage – to join him on his stall. This was his first stall.

When he was about eighteen he invited me to the opening of his second shop. He already had three market stalls. His whole little empire was staffed by my former pupils who he had educated in the arithmetic of fruit and vegetable retailing. I was surprised when I discovered that the head teacher and other members of staff thought that this boy was rather dim. By the time he was eighteen he was earning more than any of them.

At the beginning of the autumn term I was offered the post of Head of the Remedial Department with a small increase in scale and income. The generous Mr Bussey gave me five classes (one hundred and fifty children), all of whom had expected to have left school by then and most of whom were badly behaved layabouts. We were given the old secondary modern building, scheduled to be demolished at any moment, and permission to use any part of the wilderness behind. I had one other full-time teacher, an ex-journalist who at about forty thought teaching would be a more socially useful way of spending the rest of his working life. We also had the part-time services of an art teacher, a woodwork teacher and a PT teacher[70].

* * *

Our first task was to inspect our domain. I don't know, and didn't ask, where the various tools we required came from. Certainly they were not provided by the school. Shears, secateurs, scythes and other cutting equipment came forth. My tidy mind would have me start clearing near to the rest of the school but the boys persuaded me that if

[70] PT – Physical Training

we left a cordon *insanitaire* we could pursue our endeavours out of sight of anyone else. So we cut and hacked away out of the public eye. At the back of the area that we were clearing we found a small Qualcast builders hut. It was completely overgrown with shrubs and weeds. When I told the boys they could use it as a sort of club-house when the rubbish was cleared out they set to with a will. Inside, stripped of empty cement bags and other detritus, we found a table and some rough benches. Fortunately some of my class went each day to the woodwork room. The teacher there was happy to cooperate. The boys were much more enthusiastic about learning how to make benches and tables for their club house than they were about performing the somewhat sterile technical exercises which were in the regular curriculum.

I had to remember that the school leaving age had been raised in order to give children an extra year's education before sending them off into the world of work. By discussion I found out two very significant things about my charges. The first was that almost none of them had the faintest idea of any way of earning a living other than by fairly elementary buying and selling. The second was that whereas my youngest daughter would set off alone on a Saturday morning with a shilling-all-day ticket on the underground railway system and had, by the age of ten, visited virtually every station on the whole network, the London schoolchildren under my care rarely moved more than a mile or so from home. I had a list of 'target' buildings to which they were allocated. They formed little teams of four or five and had to work out the cheapest route to the destination which I gave them.

I had previously, in my own time, visited all the buildings and made a note of some significant feature that they had to find and make a note of, as proof that their mission had been successful. Every Tuesday they would go off in their little groups to find their allotted destination and make notes about its purpose, or record any other distinguishing feature. The next day I would take them class by class and they would describe their visits and how they had got there. They would bring back evidence that they had actually reached their targets, for example by making a note of something carved in stone.

I can remember one lively little group who had been sent off to find Hampton Court Palace. They found it and described the Maze – clear evidence of success. Then came the phrase in their report which brought my heart into my mouth: *'Then came the really exciting bit'*. I read on, not daring to give articulation to my misgivings. They went on: *'We went down to the river and had a paddle'*. One wonders whether any young teenagers of today would have found the acme of a day's outing, free from authority, to be having a paddle.

I realised that for this and the next activity I initiated for my ROSLA children I had to get permission for them to be out of school. I also had to get insurance cover. I will always be grateful for the kindness and efficiency of the Education Officer for Group 3 who promptly arranged both permission and insurance when he read my description of what I was intending to do.

The other problem the children faced was ignorance of more than one way of earning a living. The 'lucky' ones were those who had a relative – preferably a father – in a trade, entry to which was fiercely defended by the appropriate trade union. Printing and leather working were two trades that I came up against in those days. Apart from the restrictive practices traditionally imposed by both local employers and trade unions, the young aspirant had no knowledge of the way in which different industries were run and their entry requirements. There were no career advisory centres or courses for teachers to enable reasoned advice to be given. Since many of my charges were off the premises with permission every Tuesday, I asked whether I could also have every Tuesday off to visit companies. Permission was granted, and I wrote to the general managers of many shops, factories and other businesses within about three miles radius describing the work experience scheme I was hoping to inaugurate and asking if I could make an appointment to call for a discussion. Again, I want to express my delight at the reception my circular received.

I was not surprised that only about one in ten replied. They were mostly curious, some sceptical, but all who replied were willing to discuss what I planned. I visited and explained that the scheme was not a recruiting agency for these firms but an opportunity to give planned experience of the number of ways in which young people could earn a living. Unless there was conflict between the pupil and the firm, they would visit each employer on three successive Tuesdays and then move on, giving them an opportunity to see other ways in which young people could earn a living. In a school year each pupil would visit thirteen or fourteen different employers and I would see to it that they saw a variety of trades including offices, laboratories and a range of factories.

As soon as we had found the builder's hut the boys cleared it out, roughly furnished it and settled in to their 'discussions'. I knew that nobody in authority would pay a visit so I closed my eyes to smoking, permitted soft drinks but forbade beer or any other alcoholic beverage.

We drew up a plan of our territory and divided it into areas for specific development. In the first term I did all the work. The boys did not know the difference between a shovel and a spade. They all lived in high rise flats with no gardens. I had to teach them how to dig with a spade or fork in order to make the ground at all productive. The bottom area, furthest from the school, must have been the yard of an ancient inn. We found, for example, treasures which included used clay pipes, old buttons and medals. So we excavated our treasures, cleaned them and gradually built up an ever growing museum which we housed in one corner of our hut. All this gave rise to many lessons on the history of Shoreditch.

Gradually the boys became involved. Some, not all, learned how to dig in the soil which was revealed when the ragged undergrowth was removed and burnt. As each strip was cleared, dug and levelled the time came to decide what should be grown in it. To my surprise the almost unanimous desire was for flowers. So we managed to clear an area round the hut and to plant it, during the first autumn with bulbs. When I enquired why they wanted flowers they were unanimous that they wanted them to give regular bunches to Mrs Metcalf, the only person in authority who treated them other than as outcasts. By Christmas, although I had done most of the work of clearing, digging, levelling and planting we had a fair sized area in which we could hope for developments in the Spring.

These were two great advances, much greater than even I in my optimism had expected. First my one hundred and fifty outsiders were registering a much better attendance record than the rest of the school. And secondly, although I felt that it would be counter-productive to apply pressure, more and more of the boys were voluntarily joining in the work of ground clearing, planning the size and shape of various plots and learning how to dig and prepare for planting. The next term work continued. I still recall the astonishment with which they greeted the first emergence of green growth breaking through the earth. It motivated a great outburst in enthusiasm in learning how to dig and rake. There were lively discussions about diversification. Boys who were selling vegetables on market stalls had no idea where they came from. They were anxious to learn what plants could give quick results because they were mindful that they would be leaving it all in July and they were anxious to see results. So we allocated spaces and sowed peas and beans and prepared to buy in the market, which was just over the perimeter wall of our garden, little plants which they could hardly believe would grow into cabbages, cauliflowers and lettuces.

One day I went out into the garden which, with over a hundred helpers, had developed remarkably. We could see enough results of our labours bursting through the soil to recognise that the harder we worked the better everything looked. There was one sight which certainly I had not discussed or planned. Just beside the entrance to our garden I could just see the top of the head of a boy standing and throwing up earth in a deep hole which he had obviously dug. When he saw me he climbed out.

"What on earth is that?" I asked.

"It's a man trap", he replied. "When I've got it deep enough I will cover it lightly with sticks and spread grass on top".

"But that will be very dangerous if anyone treads on it".

"That's why I'm doing it. The other kids are jealous of what we've got going. They want to invade. Some are just curious – others intend to wreck what they can".

I called a meeting and eventually persuaded them that erecting a little fence and arranging a roster of class members to guard the entrance would be a method of protecting their property that would lead to less action by authority than – as was a distinct possibility – causing a fellow pupil to break a leg. The summer term came. We had flower beds. Boys took turns to take bouquets to Mrs Metcalf. Vegetables matured and they were each proudly permitted to take peas, beans or cabbages home to their mums. I do not know how our garden project would fit into a National Curriculum, but I know that my 150 kids learned a lot in their last year at school, and enjoyed themselves in the process.

* * *

I never tried to teach ethical values by anything other than a careful attention to example. I can remember a boy in his leaving year who was summoned to appear at Old Street magistrate's court on charges of shoplifting. As his case was to be heard on a Tuesday it was easy for me to absent myself from school and to accompany him to court. Although he pleaded Not Guilty the case against him was open and shut. The three magistrates went into a huddle to decide the boy's fate. In the visitor's area I got to my feet and asked if I could make a statement – a sort of plea in mitigation. After ascertaining that I was the boy's class teacher they asked me to swear an oath and to make my statement. I explained that I was a class teacher in a sink school in Hoxton. I had thirty boys in my class. Sixteen of them had a relative in prison. They were purposeless, having no ambition other than to seek employment, as soon as they left school, with the notorious East End villains, the Kray twins. When I started on my peroration, asking the question "Who is really guilty; the young offender or the society in which he was raised?" the chairman stopped me.

"You have made your point very clearly", he said, and once more went into a huddle with his colleagues.

"You are the first schoolteacher ever to come before this court with a few words in defence of the accused, although we have had quite a few teachers speaking for the prosecution. In the light of what you have said we will not order any punishment, although a probation order at least is indicated. We discharge him knowing that he will remain in your care."

On the way back to the school he nicked a bottle of milk off a doorstep and drank it as we walked along. I never went to court again.

* * *

Every week I dispersed one shilling and sixpence to each boy going out on a local familiarisation trip. This amounted to two pounds five shillings, drawn from the school office every Monday evening, and kept in a cashbox for distribution on Tuesday morning. One Tuesday the cash box, which had been left in my 'securely' locked little room, disappeared. I summoned the class and explained – no money, no outing. After the lunch break I went back to my room and there was the cash box, but with only six shillings and eight pence left in it. When the class assembled I explained what I had found and that I regarded the return of the cash box and some of the money as a partial victory for my relationship with the class.

"We're all sorry about this", said a self-appointed spokesman, "and we're sorry we can't get back all the dosh for you. But, believe me, he won't do it again, nor will no one else".

* * *

Within my work experience scheme boys could ask to go back for more than three visits. This often meant that they had made such a good impression that the employer was considering giving them a job when they left school. This had to be checked out, so the next time I received an application for a fourth visit I called on the employers to ask how they would react to a fourth visit.

"He's a good lad and we certainly don't dismiss the possibility of offering him employment, but do you know the real reason why he wants to keep on coming?"

When I said I had no idea, the manager went on: "He was a poor undersized little shrimp of a lad so, on his first visit, we let him into the directors' dining room. He ate two enormous lunches and we haven't had the heart to deny him the same on subsequent visits".

Who says industrialists haven't a heart?

* * *

One of the businesses which gave generously to Shoreditch School paid, as its major charitable donation of the year, for the hiring of a small ferry boat in which the whole school could go on a day trip to Boulogne. On our arrival in my first year I noticed that all the staff made a rapid beeline for a café and ensconced themselves under big sunshades, abandoning their classes to their own devices. I set off up the hill away from the dock, pointing out places of interest, translating simple notices and doing my best to answer questions. The boys had been told that they didn't have to stay with me, but most of them did. We visited the street market and the cathedral, ate French bread and cheese for lunch and eventually, having had a good day's outing, returned to the quayside. The other teachers were still at the same café when we got back. My class were sent in an orderly fashion to round up the others. Eventually we got them all back on board.

As soon as we were clear of land I bagged a cabin and lined up my class. I explained that there were some things they might have bought in France that it was illegal to bring into England and that I wanted to ensure that they got into no trouble. They emptied their pockets and bags one by one. They had all got small presents for mothers or siblings. What I had suspected, however, was justified. Half of them had acquired lethal-looking flick knives.

"These are illegal in England and all returning school parties are searched for knives and any other illegal purchases on arrival. I don't want any of you to get into trouble. The safest thing to do if you have bought a flick knife is to chuck it overboard."

With great reluctance they did. The whole school party was searched by Customs on arrival. One teacher appeared before magistrates the next day and was fined for not preventing his charges committing a criminal offence.

16

I suppose it is possible for two people who are, in temperament and aspiration, diametrically opposed to live in harmony together. I have already recorded how Gwen and I first met. She was a very beautiful girl. I fell for her absolutely. However, my service during World War Two and my five years as a Member of Parliament contributed to a steady growing apart.

I do not make a virtue of it, but I am a totally non-materialistic human being. I do not own anything. My marital flat and its contents were made over to my first wife. Possessions which were very personal to me, gifts from constituents when I was an M.P., for example, were all included in detail in Gwen's will. Occasionally I have recognised a former possession in the home of one of my daughters, and mentioned it. To their credit they have immediately offered restitution, which I have declined. I instinctively shun possessions. When I remarried, after Gwen's divorce and subsequent death in a road accident, both the house in Hornchurch and later in Couze, France were registered in the name of Ivy, my beloved second wife. Concomitant with my rejection of ownership was an inability to enter into undertakings that would make money. My first wife, however, could never accept her position as the wife of a poor and unambitious man.

Unfortunately I had attained roles which conferred upon me a singular credit-worthy status. As a Wing Commander in the R.A.F. and as an M.P. this credit-worthiness was readily transferred to my wife. Especially in Chelmsford, which I represented in Parliament, the best shops were only too ready to give her credit. The first I knew that she had such facilities was when the bills began to appear. The proprietors of the two main shops in Chelmsford were both youngish men with whom I was reasonably friendly.

There had been, I seem to remember, a major fire in the centre of Chelmsford. Both the principle furniture suppliers, one a private shop and the other a cooperative furniture store, were gutted. Each was insured separately from the other and each was having great difficulty in exacting a promise of recompense adequate to pay for new building and for replacement of stock, the cost of which – with furniture in a repository and a shop – is devastating. They both declined to accept the offer made by their insurers and both came, independently of one another, to me to ask advice. I am, of course, not a lawyer, but I managed to get the principals of the two companies, who were at first at loggerheads, to meet with me together with legal advisers, who specialised in insurance claims. The two claimants made a joint claim, based upon the joint incidence of the fire, and were awarded between them considerably more than the sum of their individual claims. I was therefore on excellent personal terms with the owners and managers of these concerns. By word of mouth, through such organisations as the local Chamber of Commerce, my reputation as a sympathetic aid to local businessmen in distress, rose dramatically.

A by-product of this was the ease with which my wife obtained virtually unlimited credit. I saw the relevant proprietors, partly to explain why early payment of the credit accounts was impossible but also to stop any further credit being granted. This did not come into effect without a great deal of acrimony within my marriage but it worked – with one exception. Through the Business and Professional Women's Association, of which she was now President, Gwen knew all the ladies of influence in local commerce. One of them was senior saleslady of the best dress shop. The autumn Mayor's Ball was coming up. Gwen had to have a new dress. Her friend obliged her. As I had reluctantly and painfully stopped credit, it was in order for me to refuse to pay. Eventually my friendship with the proprietor prevailed and the dress went back, but not until after the Mayor's Ball.

* * *

The last thing I want to do is to bad-mouth anybody, especially the person I married and by whom I became the father of four splendid and interesting daughters. My first-born, christened Anne Elizabeth, was born on December 13th 1938. Amongst my neighbours was a Mrs Ash, who had only one child – a son who clearly would never make her a grandmother. Mrs Ash was devoted to the baby Anne, and seized every opportunity to push her in her pram for walks around Wallington, as far as Croydon. One day, passing the main Croydon store, Mrs Ash saw in the window that, together with the local newspaper, they were looking for beautiful children. Their search took the form of a photographic competition. Without our knowledge Mrs Ash proudly presented Anne as an entry in the under six months baby girl class. The first we knew about this was when we read in the local paper that our daughter had been chosen as the most beautiful girl baby in South East England.

It was soon clear that she was not only beautiful enough to win the under six months prize, but also that she was very bright. I think my first intimation of quite how bright came when she was just under five years old. By then I was a pilot in Bomber Command, flying Lancasters on operations throughout Europe. For elementary reasons of security one did not discuss, not even with one's nearest and dearest, where we were going in some future operation. But operations which were past and had been written up in newspapers or discussed on the radio could be mentioned at home. We were sitting talking, my wife and I, in front of a sitting room fire. Anne was on the floor, lying in her favourite position, on her tummy, reading a book. The Germans had occupied most of western Europe and were driving towards the Channel ports with a view to invading Britain. They had made a strong tank attack towards Calais which had been driven back by the combined efforts of the British Army and the R.A.F. Anne was obviously listening to my report to Gwen of my role in the victorious repulse which rendered Calais and the other Channel ports, at least temporarily, safe from conquest. Suddenly a small voice from the floor said:

"I know about Calais. It is where William of Normandy raised the troops with which he invaded England".

On questioning, she showed us the reference in the book she was reading which, if I remember rightly, had no direct connection with recent history nor with a frustrated Nazi invasion.

The next few years were war years in which I saw little of my family. Gwen thought, probably with reason, that the standard of scholarship shown by the staff and pupils at the village school at Boreham was not very high, and unlikely to be challenging to a very bright child. Enquiries were made and Gwen decided, after a visit to the school, that the little private school named St Cedd's, in Chelmsford, was the best bet for our eldest. As it turned out, St Cedd's was not a very good proposition. It was some time, months if not years, before we discovered that not all the staff were qualified to teach.

Anne went on a scholarship to Christ's Hospital. There she went from strength to strength, and eventually gained entry to Lady Margaret Hall, Oxford. I was an officer at Halton, only a few miles from Oxford, which enabled us to visit frequently and for Anne to come to Officers'

Mess functions. Here she was a great social success. She was quite small, slender and very pretty. I gained great credit in the eyes of many young officers – it was a training centre for young graduates who had been called up under the National Service Act – for being father to such an attractive daughter. However, she fell for a young Oxford student, Peter Smith. Apparently for B.A. final examinations candidates took ten papers. I understand that Peter achieved an A grade in the nine papers concerned with the great literature of the past – Shakespeare, Milton etc – but failed the tenth paper, which was on the origins of the English language. Unfortunately the chairman of the examining board that year taught linguistics and wanted to withhold Peter's degree on the grounds that he had failed an essential element of the course. A compromise was reached. The universities had many students who were outstanding for skills other than the academic. Rowers, runners, players of ball games represented the university without quite reaching the appropriate academic standard even for a third class degree. They were given a fourth class degree. An intervention from the literature don secured one of these degrees for Peter, not for athletic skills but because he spent much time in successfully producing student plays and editing student magazines.

Anne and Peter both became teachers at public schools. Anne went on to a very distinguished career as a teacher, eventually becoming the Founder Principal of Croydon's first Sixth Form College. This was so successful that parents from the neighbouring borough of Bromley sought to get their children into the school.

The couple parented two very interesting children. The elder, Patrick, shared with me the 'distinction' of being the only member of the extended family who is not a university graduate. However, he has shown a remarkable knowledge of and skill in the many interesting by-ways of the insurance industry. He works very long hours, motoring many miles a week in connection with his work, much of which is advisory and consultative. He is married to Vicki. They have two children, Annie Grace and Rebecca, and give every appearance of a successful, modern family.

Anne's second child is also called Victoria. She went to university and gained a good degree in English before deciding a year later that she wanted to become a lawyer.. Her mother had taught the daughter of a local solicitor, who took Vicki in whilst she studied and did the specialist training to become a solicitor. Apparently it is not possible to qualify without the experience of working in a solicitor's office. Eventually she qualified and applied to join the Treasury Solicitor's Department of the Civil Service. On acceptance she worked representing the department of the Home Office responsible for Immigration. She has subsequently moved to represent the Office of Fair Trading.

Peter did not continue for teaching for his whole career. He became a member of the teachers' trade union which is now called the Association of Teachers and Lecturers (A.T.L.). He took over the editorship of his union's magazine with great success. When a vacancy occurred, he became Assistant General Secretary and negotiated a merger with a sister union. On the retirement of the General Secretary Peter was promoted, and held the office of General Secetary himself until his own retirement in 2003. He was appointed a Companion of the British Empire in the same year.

* * *

Susan, our second daughter, was born on May 18 1941. She was in many ways the opposite of Anne. Whereas Anne had a head of dark curls which framed a lively, laughing face, Susan was a blonde with long, straight, very fine hair. This lent itself to being brushed straight down, parted and plaited with a coloured ribbon bow at the end of each plait. Unfortunately the hair was so fine that the plaits became unplaited and the bows fell off. Sadly both plaits did not fall out at the same time and I retain the strong image of Susan with half her hair still in the plait with a ribbon at the end and the other half loose and dishevelled. She also had a thoughtful, intent look on her face most of the time, an aspect which still persists. Like Anne, Susan went to St Cedd's where she had experiences which seemed to alter her character and condition her throughout her life until, at the age of about sixty, she found her particular niche. She became a very successful lay reader in the Church of England and established a reputation for wisdom and sanctity which is still with her.

At St Cedd's Anne had been the star pupil. Bright, eager, curious about learning, very good looking and in every way the image of the 'teacher's pet'. Susan entered the school a year or so later. I have always felt that she was just as intelligent as her sister. However the staff constantly referred, in a disparaging fashion, to her eagerness to volunteer answers in class and to her general air of awkwardness and untidiness. Susan became stubborn. Determined not to let her natural intelligence be suffocated she worked hard but seemed to know that she could never be regarded as being as bright as her sister. So she stifled what she undoubtedly knew and began to be regarded as a bit of an eccentric.

Some years later she was marginally awarded a first class honours degree. The examination board sent for her to report for a confirmatory viva. She rang and said she couldn't come on the appointed day. This was unprecedented. The board asked why she couldn't come, and she replied that she was getting married, and that getting married was more important than the class of her degree. So they brought the viva forward by one day. When she appeared before the examiners she was shiny-eyed and paid little attention to their questions. She was rewarded with a 2.1 degree.

When Anne was about nine years old a local headmaster. George Mills, suggested that she might be entered for a scholarship to Christ's Hospital. The girls' school, conveniently for us, was at Hertford. She succeeded brilliantly and began her secondary school career as a boarder at Christ's Hospital. Two years later Susan followed her. Christ's Hospital is an interesting establishment. Supported strongly by charitable investment it was, and still is, able to take into consideration parental income in order to set fees appropriate to parents' ability to pay. I had at the time one serious criticism. Every morning at assembly the children thanked the Almighty for the generosity and charity of the Founders and Governors of the school. The children were daily reminded that they were the recipients of that charity, for which they should always be grateful.

Susan recounted later that one of her happiest memories of early childhood involved being in bed with influenza. The bedroom light is out, but it is not dark. There is an oil heater burning. As she lies in bed she can see the flickering light shining up to the ceiling through the lattice work holes in the top of the heater. She is wrapped in my lambs wool lined flying jacket. Bliss to an eight year old.

Susan married Bryn Williams, an Oxford colleague. They were blessed with two children, both high achievers, although not following similar career paths. Although Bryn was entirely raised in England, their son was named Gareth – Gareth Williams would be a splendid name were he to be selected to play rugby for Wales. However, his future turned out to be academic rather than sporting. I can remember a long conversation I had with Gareth on the day of Patrick's wedding. Gareth was just sixteen, and already committed to the study of history. During our conversation I mentioned my own theory that the best evidence historians can use is found in contemporary primary sources. These include, of course, published writings, books, articles in learned journals, letters – preferably to other historians or to newspapers like the Times. These letters are, by their very nature, written by biased authors. General officers write their memoirs in which they praise their own successes and tend to blame others for their failures. Politicians also leave much testimony of their activity and influence for the good of the country. The best written history tends to be based upon evidence left by people in high places who can rarely be accused of impartiality. Gareth agreed and told me that his ambition was to select a period of history and write a completely impartial analysis of the forces and decisions which obtained at the time. He left school for university and went on to achieve a doctorate for his post graduate researches. His selected period covered the Middle Ages, that period ill-taught in school until brought back to life by the excitements of *1066 And All That*. So Gareth had his doctorate in a period where there was a great need for new sources. He was appointed to the appropriate department of the British Museum and became curator of medieval coins and medals. Appropriately, he met and married another specialist, a Canadian philosopher, Michele Friend. Sadly there were no vacancies at British universities for Michele's specialism. She could find employment only in America, at Washington University. The marriage has had to be conducted for some years with the wide waters of the Atlantic separating them for much of the year.

Susan and Bryn's elder child was a girl. When it came to naming her it gave rise to considerable discussion and consultation around the family. Bryn was anxious that she should be named after a Shakespearian character. It became evident that Shakespeare's young ladies were, on the whole, rather unfortunate in their careers. Undoubtedly the connotations of Regan and Goneril would be unacceptable, and who would want to chain a growing girl to the sad fate of Ophelia? One bright light shone out from the pages of the Bard: Cordelia. As a very young girl, Susan had believed that the berries of the rowan tree were a specific against witches. Although it is likely that she abandoned this belief by the time she became mother of a daughter, she and Bryn settled on an amalgamation of their interests and their daughter was christened Rowan Cordelia.

Both Cordelia and Gareth were highly intelligent. Gareth's intelligence was academic although it is of interest to me, with my political background, that he has had a second role in the British Museum. For some years he was the spokesman for, and coordinator of, the various trade unions amongst the staff of the Museum, a job which gave him much satisfaction. Cordelia – who has now adopted her other name, and is called Rowan – has a strongly developed religious bent. She is an authority on the life and teachings of St Francis of Assisi, having spent seven years as a novice with an Anglican Order of Franciscan Sisters. She left the Order some years ago, and has just completed her second degree at Cambridge – the first was in German, this is a theology degree – having been accepted as an ordinand in the Church of England. She is hoping to be accepted to complete a PhD, as well as becoming a minister in the Church of England: in 2005 she was ordained Deacon. She is a pamphleteer of conviction, and highly regarded in Franciscan circles.

* * *

I have one or two lively recollections of my children when they were very young. The first occurred just before Christmas in 1947. The favourite radio series in our household was called I.T.M.A.[71] In it there was a female character called Mona Lott. She had two catchphrases – "Can I do you now, Sir?" and "What me? In my state of health?" The other influence on them at that time of year was that they frequently went to Nativity plays and clearly Deborah, aged three, was particularly impressed by them.

One day I stopped outside their nursery door, which held a glass panel, enabling me to see what was going on inside. Deborah was sitting in a chair and Susan, aged six, came in carrying a stick with a silver star on the end. She was an angel.

"Hail Mary!" said the angel, waving her want. "You are going to have a baby!" To which Mary (aged three) replied: "What, me? In my state of health?"

The other incident gave a clear indication of their respective interests. Our cat gave birth to four kittens. The girls were told that each could name one. The year was, I seem to remember, 1950. Anne, aged twelve, called her kitten Leonardo da Vinci. Susan, at nine, preferred William Shakespeare. Deborah, full of ballet aged six, wanted Margot Fonteyn. And the one year old Caroline chose Dunkles.

* * *

Just after the end of the war I received an unannounced call at my house in Boreham. It was a young Polish doctor. He was still in the Polish army but could not rise above the rank of corporal because he was

---

[71] *It's That Man Again*

Jewish. He had come to ask for help. He was married to a German Jewish girl who was interned in a camp. If she could get into the country he could look after her. I took all his particulars and sought an interview with the Minister of State responsible for the British Zone in defeated Germany. His name was, if I remember rightly, Harry Hynd. In a startlingly short space of time he secured the release of Greta and she came to England. She and her husband came to see us at Boreham and were astonished when I said that I was a public servant and could not accept payment for doing what was only my duty.

In the Spring of the next year they called again. Greta brought gifts for my wife and daughters. She herself was a designer and maker of artificial jewellery. They apologised that all their assets were in France and that exchange controls would not permit them to bring anything to England. So they had booked a month for two adults and three children in a boarding house at a village on the coast of France called Berck Plage. They had paid for everything but we would have to manage the cost of our own transport as they could not pay for it in France. We, of course, accepted and agreed a date.

The date came. It was a gamble. We had an address in Berck Plage but no address for my Polish friend and his wife. The journey was a great adventure. One of my Chelmsford political friends offered to drive us to Dover to catch the one thirty boat to Calais from where we would catch a train to Rouen and change to another train to Berck. There was a colossal traffic jam at Ashford. Half the road was up for repairs. We were held up for nearly an hour. We arrived at Dover at one forty. We had missed our boat. Fortunately our friend with the car had not left us. There was a two forty five ferry for Boulogne leaving from Folkestone. We sped across southern England and arrived with some time to spare. The time came for boarding but alas! the boat was not taking passengers. The train for the ferry had broken down on the way from London and the boat had to wait until the train came in. Instead of the one thirty at Dover, or two forty five at Folkestone we embarked and left Folkestone for Boulogne at five forty five p.m.

The war had only been over for a few months and the French railway system was still blacked out. The only sign which one could read on the station was a small board illuminated by a lamp with the name of the station on it. It was by the exit. We knew that we had to change at Rouen, so we asked how many stops. Rouen Tintillery: four stops. We got aboard. The train started and pulled up again, still at the same platform. We did not know that this was the first stop – from Boulogne

Maritime to Boulogne Ville. We took off again and stopped twice at small stations. "One more to go and then our stop", we thought. We stopped. One. As we drew out we saw by a small light over the ticket collector's booth the sign Rouen Tintillery. We had arrived unaware at our destination and were now being carried off into the night.

The train stopped at Arras at ten thirty p.m. Here we were, in France, with three small children late at night, and lost. We found a friendly railway official and explained that out boat was late and that in the dark we had not realised that Boulogne Maritime and Boulogne Ville, although well within sight of each other, were in fact two stations. He endorsed our tickets so that we would have no difficulty the next morning and told us that the train would leave at ten a.m.

"Come early", he said, then told us to follow the high wall that we could see outside the station, "and you will find somewhere to sleep for the night". We duly found a tall, thin building which was still open. We were greeted by a concierge and when we explained what had happened and that we needed a room with two large beds, one for two adults and the other for three now completely exhausted children, he took up a board, with a handle, on which were printed the numbers of the rooms and a price against each. He pointed to a room number, I have forgotten what the price was in francs, but I remember it worked out at about seven shillings and sixpence. I thought it was seven and six each, so I counted out one pound seventeen shillings and sixpence, which I pushed over to him. He shoved most of it back. It was not seven and six each, but seven and six for the room. In the morning we got up early. There were facilities for washing, so we all freshened up, went out and found a café, had our first French breakfast and went to the station. It was about nine twenty five. "When the train comes in find a seat and save a place for me. I'll go and deal with the baggage".

The platform started to fill up with people. I later discovered that it was a *ferie* (bank holiday) and in France everybody who can goes to the seaside on a *ferie*. As the train pulled in I saw that the guard's van was at the front, so I rushed to the front of the train with our luggage. I had opened the guard's van door when a small official wearing shirt, waistcoat, slacks and a red tie – his uniform, I presumed – came running up.

"C'est interdit!"[72] he shouted.

---

[72] "It's forbidden!"

"But we are English visitors."

"Down with English visitors!" he spat.

"But I am a Member of Parliament."

"Down with Members of Parliament!" He spat again.

"But I am a Socialist."

"Down with Socialists! I am a Communist." He spat once more.

"But I am a British pilot come back to see France."

"R.A.F?" he queried.

"Oui."

"Vive le R.A.F!" and he picked up our baggage and carried it to the guard's van, opened the door, dusted a box inside with a cloth he took out of his pocket and carefully ushered us in.

We thus arrived at Berck and found our accommodation a good twenty four hours before the telegram arrived to say that we would be late. As soon as we arrived and were greeted by Monsieur Devoucoux, our host, Anne and Susan wanted to see the beach. So we asked for and consumed a quick snack and made for a gap in the sand dunes which, we were told, would lead us to the beach. When we got there and saw the vast expanse of sand uncovered for many hundred yards – for the tide was right out – Gwen and flopped, exhausted, onto the sand. Anne and Deborah went off to explore together and Susan began her inevitable investigation of little pools and other features.

When we woke up it was about five o'clock. The tide had come in but there was still a good expanse of sand. People had put up nets and were playing handball, football or other games. There were a lot of people about. Quite near the entrance was a portable kiosk with a loud speaker on top. Inside a man from time to time gave information about the weather and other points of interest. After about half an hour there was no sign of Susan, so I went over to the kiosk and asked the man if he could broadcast a message:

LOST. SMALL ENGLISH GIRL, LONG FAIR HAIR IN PLAITS, PROBABLY UNDONE. ONLY WEARING BLUE *SLIPS*.[73]

He sent out the message and promised to repeat it every few minutes. After about an hour a policeman came up and told us to get back to Monsieur Devoucoux's and wait. Another half hour. I went to the police station. All policemen had been taken off traffic and other duties.

[73] *Slips* – French for knickers

At seven forty five around the corner came a policeman carrying Susan piggy-back. She had wandered nearly two miles away and had gone to a group of people to ask if they could help her. They couldn't understand her and she couldn't understand them, so she went to the kiosk when up came the rescuing policeman and brought her to us. An English voice in the crowd which followed her called out, "Don't worry, love. Your mum and dad will soon come and find you".

For the rest of our stay policemen would halt all traffic, come across and shake hands and ask, "Lost any children lately?"

* * *

Our third daughter, Deborah Jane, was born on February 3rd 1944. She was a small-boned, dainty baby. My impression, undoubtedly somewhat exaggerated, was that she was born dancing. Certainly by the age of two she seemed to dance more than walk or run. She was as light as thistledown. Like Anne and Susan she went to St Cedd's. She was a very merry child, much liked by all the neighbours. In Christmas pantomimes and other activities in the Village Hall Deborah was delighted to give a little dance which was much appreciated. While she was small I went back into the RAF and was posted to Halton, in Buckinghamshire. We had kept in touch with friends in Boreham and, one day, a neighbour – Cecily Pelly – came to us with an extremely generous proposition. She had found out that the Arts Educational School, which specialised in dance training, was at Tring about ten miles from where we were living. Knowing that our financial circumstances would not permit us to do so ourselves, she said that she would pay for Deborah to go to A.E.S. Before accepting that she should meet the whole cost of a child at boarding school, although I think she could probably have afforded it, we applied to Essex County Council for a grant. The council were not used to giving a grant to attend a school for dancing. Debbie had to appear before them and give a demonstration. This she did, and won them over. She received her grant.

The Arts Educational School was in a former Rothschild mansion at Tring. The patroness was Margot Fonteyn, and the actual dancing tutelage seemed excellent. It was as though the management was not concerned about formal classroom education. The headmistress was a dull lady, wife of a Methodist parson. She appeared to be obliged to permit theatrical training, with much of which she apparently disagreed, to take precedence of time and space over academic activity. Periodically the Fine Arts staff would be called upon to get the students to produce works of art to dress the hall, a massive entrance to the mansion, for visitors' day.

We were telephoned urgently one day. Could we come at once. Deborah had submitted a vast painting, about fifteen feet by six feet, which she wanted to exhibit in the centre of the hall. It was her representation of Lucifer, the fallen angel, captured during his fall from Heaven to the nether regions. The top half was bathed in golden light. The face and head were beautiful. There were angelic wings spread in the golden light. But as one's eyes moved down the painting it was clear that the light was fading. Clothing was more sombre; more grey. Finally the grey and black became diffused with dark red and orange. The bottom of the legs and feet were covered in flames. All around was the lurid light of Hell. Lucifer was falling; his head still in Heaven but his legs and feet already in Hades.

The Headmistress met us and, without showing us the painting, described it as obscene, blasphemous and disgusting, and announced that she was considering asking us to take Deborah away that very day.

"She constitutes", said the headmistress, "a serious moral threat to the whole school".

As mildly as I could, I remonstrated with her for announcing her verdict without producing the evidence or hearing any explanation. Very reluctantly the much shaken woman produced the offending painting. I thought it was brilliant. The concept was not one which I would have chosen, but she had planned it with a fine sense of artistic balance and executed it with considerable skill. It had meant a lot to her, and to have it rejected on spiritual grounds by someone with a religious background was heartbreaking. I expressed myself very strongly that it was sad that a woman who could not see the high religious content of the child's work should be in charge of her educational and moral welfare. I would be taking her from the school in *my* time. She would be withdrawn at the end of term. What I knew, because Deborah had confided it to me, was that the school had no more to offer her. She was growing rapidly. The little fairy was now a biggish teenager, growing in the Millington mould. She still wanted a stage career, but felt that dancing would not be her professional metier. The academic or formal school teaching was very inadequate, being held to be subordinate in importance to dancing, and only one form of dancing at that – classical ballet.

She admitted that she was in the habit of some rather naughty practices. After they were all tucked down in the dormitories, she and one or two like-minded friends would quickly dress and meet by arrangement boys from Berkhamstead Grammar School. She also took to climbing on to the roof of the school building. (It was ironic that some time before we had been called in because she had fractured a wrist, tripping over a fallen log in the grounds.) She was now nearly sixteen and keen to make a start, if possible, in the theatre.

At that time I was quite friendly with Tom Driberg who, I knew, was himself friendly with the avant-garde producer of plays at the Stratford East Theatre, Joan Littlewood. Tom gave Deborah an introduction, and she went to an interview. She was first asked if she was still a virgin. Startled at such an unexpected question Deborah, who held a self-image of being a rather progressive and risqué fifteen year old, denied having lost her virginity.

"Have you had an affair with another girl?"

Again, indignant denial.

"Come back and see me when you have had some experience of life".

So Debbie went back to the London branch of the Arts Educational Trust until, at quite a young age, she got a place and went to R.A.D.A.[74] She left home and moved in with three male students from R.A.D.A. She was much in love with a young Jewish boy, Stanley Lebor. They were told by his mother that she forbade him to marry a *shiksa*[75], but would welcome any child of the union as long as the child was brought up as a Jew. The tie of the Jewish mother was stronger than Stanley's love for Deborah, who refused the conditions, and broke off the attachment. She subsequently married Nigel Anthony, another actor.

It was a strong and productive relationship. They had three boys – Sam, Ben and Tom. Deborah gave them the shortest possible names, as she did not want their names to be diminished. Deborah did not have an extensive career in acting. She was too busy being a good mum and housewife. The union with Nigel broke up. She then spent some years following an attraction to the unorthodox end of extreme left-wing politics[76]. Much of her time was spent selling far-Left literature outside the local Underground station and in pubs in central London. Later she was admitted to a teacher training college where she met her second

[74] The Royal Academy of Dramatic Art
[75] Yiddish for non Jewish girl
[76] She became active in the Workers Revolutionary Party, the W.R.P

husband, Simon Edwards. He began their marriage in a somewhat unorthodox fashion by playing in a cricket match on their wedding afternoon. Their union was much shorter than her marriage with Nigel.

Finally, as a trained teacher, driven I suspect by the social conscience which was already there but probably enlarged during her ultra-Left period, she opted for the teaching of children with special needs. A combination of her dramatic skills, a marvellously relaxed manner with her students and her innate intelligence ensured that she became a great success. I can remember when she was a student I was working in an all-girls school. I was the only man on the staff because no one else could be found to tackle the under-educated and badly behaved majority. She volunteered to come and take one of my classes. I was delighted to accept, and left her to it. When the time came for the bell to ring to mark the end of the period I went back into my classroom. Deborah was sitting on a table, swinging her legs – not provocatively, but in a completely relaxed manner. The girls, probably not much her junior, had pushed back their chairs and were gathered round in a rough circle. Deborah was elegantly smoking a cigarette. The girls were obviously fascinated, and were reluctant to break up the lesson. Except for the fag, it augured well for her future in education.

Moving successfully in the special education circuit she met a steady, intelligent Geordie, Tom Greener. Tom was headmaster of a special school but soon left to join the inspectorate. This involved travelling a great deal and visiting schools and colleges. They got on well together and were eventually married. They shared their employment in special education in common. Tom was splendidly opposite to Deborah in temperament. She was volatile; he was balanced and careful. They got on well, she particularly enjoying and impressing his family in the North East of England. At one stage she decided to transfer from the classroom to an administrative post in education. I think she found this boring and exhausting so she applied for and obtained early retirement. Deborah had a small house in Putney. When she retired, she and Tom leased a house in Dorset, in much more idyllic surroundings.

Whether it is the change from urgent London living to the gentler life in the Dorset countryside, or her pleasure at being able to give up the administrative life she found so irksome, Deborah became a more relaxed woman. Always generous by nature she has become even more so. Every visit is accompanied by a box of books, all new and up to date, and all chosen with an idea of the taste of the recipients. There are also reports of her great generosity, not only to us but to other elderly people in her orbit. She and Tom are always welcome to pay us visits, and it is the warmth of their greeting which is a great deal more delightful than any gifts they bring, much as these are appreciated.

Susan, Caroline, Anne and Deborah – early 1950s

Our youngest was born on August 4th 1949 and christened Caroline Sarah. We always remember the date of the late Queen Mother's birthday. It was the same date as Caroline's – but in a very different year.

The early part of Caroline's life was quite different from that of her sisters. We had no settled home. Part of it was spent in a sordid central London pub; part in an almost as sordid boarding house. However, we escaped to 6 Battledean Road and did not, I think, dislike our life in Islington. Caroline had started school at the Christopher Hatton Primary School at Mount Pleasant. At the earliest possible opportunity she moved on to Grey Coat Hospital grammar school in Westminster. It was with some pride that I saw reflected in her some of my own early academic prowess. However, when I reached sixteen I was kicked out of my home and had to earn a living. When Caroline reached sixteen she had also reached the standard qualifying her to apply for university entrance. Both her elder sisters went to Oxford colleges. Caroline did not want to follow in their footsteps.[77] There were several

---

[77] *Just as well! Having failed Latin O level twice, Oxford would not have had me. CM*

universities being formed. The one with most publicity was Sussex – because the twin daughters of Labour Minister Douglas Jay were going there. Caroline chose York. She was, however, only sixteen and did not wish to go to university at such a young age. She asked for typing lessons and then to go and live for a while in Paris. The lessons were easy, Paris less so, but when we discussed the problem with a friend who also attended St Batholomew's Church in the City of London, John Mates, he said that his mother lived in a big house in Paris. He was sure that she would be happy to let a room – "in return for some light dusting" – to the young lady whom her son assured her was a chorister in a London church choir, and who had a most beautiful voice.

I remember hearing Caroline sing at a Christmas Eve service at St Barts. The choir lined up out of sight of the congregation and prepared to start the procession towards the altar and the choir stalls. Everybody was hushed and awaiting the first notes of the processional hymn. As though by magic there came the first pure note of the first verse of *Once in Royal David's City*. It was a magical moment.

Whilst still at primary school Caroline developed an interest and considerable skill in the playing of the recorder. The recorder is the musical instrument most commonly taught in our primary schools. However well taught, not every child becomes a maestro. Caroline, however, showed an early aptitude which has developed and persisted to this day. Recorders come in a range of three registers. She acquired instruments of each pitch and sought out like-minded friends with whom she could play in consort. At the University of York she met a music student, Michael Robinson. She is still playing recorder and piano pieces with him, although Michael has become one of the most skilled and reputable of investigative reporters who appear from time to time on television.

When she started at the new university of York she joined a few earnest young men who wanted to start a college newspaper. She and her friend David Vincent became the editors – as well as the typists. Later they became co-editors of the University newspaper. It is difficult to itemise the origins of Caro's interest in public affairs. She was the daughter of an ex-M.P. and brought up in a household where current affairs were regularly discussed. She had lived abroad. Her perspective was broader than that of the straight-from-school student. The topic of explaining Town and Gown to one another became an important and ongoing feature of the newspaper she edited.

Caroline applied to the B.B.C for its new journalist training course, and was accepted before her final exams. It is typical of her good fortune that during the summer months prior to taking up her appointment in September she received a mock apologetic letter from the Personnel Department of the BBC deploring the fact that there had been a review of salaries since her appointment had been announced and that she would be receiving a different salary from that stated in the contract; graduate trainees' salaries were to be enhanced by a significant percentage which made her starting salary more than mine, her father, ex-Wing Commander, ex M.P. and for several years a qualified teacher.

Thus Caroline began her BBC career. She went through the process of producing both for television and radio. Eventually she transferred to the management side of the BBC, shot up the ranks and finished up as deputy to the legendary Liz Forgan. Upon retirement on pension she undertook several minor jobs until, like Sir Walter Raleigh, she became an important servant of the crown. In 2004 she took up appointment as non-executive Chair of the North West London Strategic Health Authority. [78] A big job for my little girl. Sir Walter would be as pleased as I am proud!

---

[78] An umbrella NHS organisation with the remit to manage the performance of eighteen NHS bodies (hospital, mental health and primary care trusts) in eight Boroughs in North West London.

17

It was, I thought, time I moved on. It was clear that in the ordinary life of a teacher I now had no hope of further promotion. Application had been made for one or two headships. I did not receive the courtesy of a rejection slip or even acknowledgement of any of my applications. It was clear that only some senior post which nobody fancied would meet my requirements. There were two such posts being advertised at the same time. The first was for a deputy headship of a new comprehensive school. It was made clear that the new head teacher, a well-known Communist called Max Morris, was looking for a deputy who was committed to the comprehensive principle and would share the heavy burden of resisting the hostility of the members of the staff of the grammar school which had been closed and of the pupils transferred to the new comprehensive. A second virtue would be some degree of political background which would enable the appointee to understand Max Morris's philosophy, even if not wholly sharing it.

The second vacancy was a new appointment being made in the London Borough of Newham. Newham had recently opened a new Teachers' Centre, expressly for the distribution of experimental resources and the training of teachers in the new Nuffield mathematics. Funds had now become available to expand the Teachers' Centre to an all-subject, all-age centre for in-service training[79]. The Schools' Council had had a project in which developments in in-service training could be tried out. One of the recommendations was the establishment of a Teachers' Centre in which the expertise of established teachers could be developed and shared. Clearly the small number of authorities which had established Nuffield Maths Centres had a head start. Newham advertised for a Leader of Curriculum Studies. Although it was not made specific it was taken for granted that the Leader would have a special concern for the secondary sector, although the appointing panel had an equal number of

---

[79] The Nuffield project was specifically only for primary schools

inspectors of primary schools and secondary schools on it.

I applied for both appointments. The interviews were on successive days, the Max Morris interview the day before the Teachers' Centre appointment. To my amazement I was offered both jobs. I much preferred the Newham post, so I accepted it and telephoned Mr Wyeth, the Chief Education Officer of – I seem to remember – Kilburn, withdrawing my acceptance of the deputy headship. I received a stinging letter from him in which, sarcastically, he hoped I would give more loyalty to my new employers than I had to him. I showed the letter to Mr Openshaw, Chief Education Officer of Newham, who burst out laughing.

"Old Wyeth", he said, "was always a stuffy old bugger. How can you owe loyalty to somebody for whom you have never taken up employment? Think nothing of it."

* * *

The Teachers' Centre at Newham was housed on the top floor of the New City Primary School, of which the Infants' Department occupied the ground floor and the Juniors the first floor. At the appropriate time the candidates assembled to be briefed as to what the job would consist of, and to meet the only other member of staff already appointed.

I can see her now as she was when I first set eyes on her. In a room seemingly full of applicants for the newly created role of Leader of Curriculum Studies, all male, all – according to my memory – at least six feet tall. All extrovert enough to be applying for a post the precise terms of which had never been determined. Amongst them, smiling a warm welcome, was a vision of loveliness: Ivy. Quite tall for a woman but not so tall as to intimidate a mere male. Soberly dressed in a navy blue suit with a velvet collar. A knee length skirt revealing as beautiful a pair of legs as one could wish to see. Thirty seven years later and the sight of them makes me catch my breath in admiration. Mr Wyeth and Mr Morris were totally dismissed from my considerations. This was where I wanted to work. This was the companion with whom I wanted to work.

Ivy was doing what she has always done superbly, at work or at home. She was making a group of strangers feel welcome. I experienced what the French call a *coup de foudre* – a thunderbolt, a flash of lightning. I still feel it. I fell in love, a condition from which I have never deviated. Some years passed before I could bring myself to declare my feelings. I was astonished and delighted to find that they were reciprocated. Times were different in those days. Further years had to pass before we were – o frabjous day! – married in 1975.

The best basis for a successful marriage is community of interest. It was thrilling to discover that we knew the same music-hall songs, that we laughed at the same jokes, that we read the same books, that we were bored by the same politicians and found the same people pompous. Subsequently Ivy became a college lecturer. We had a great joint interest in education. Above all was the joy we shared in spending much of our long educational holidays driving about France and Western Europe.

Ivy and Ernest

At first we were content to follow minor roads and ignore the auto-routes which seemed to us too much like the main trunk roads in England. We had with us a number of old maps, of France and of Europe. Each evening we inked in the routes we had followed that day. Our maps became like spiders' webs. We were often amazed to find ourselves crossing a route that seemed familiar, only to discover that we had driven it five years previously. Looking back now, the sun always seems to have been shining. Each newly discovered region filled us with joy. We began to feel that we would like to get to know certain parts more intimately. We needed a centre from which to sally forth in various directions.

For Easter 1982 Ivy and I went by public transport to Paris. We stayed in a three-star hotel, but although it rained continuously for three days, no heating was put on in the hotel before six o'clock in the evening. We had a thoroughly miserable time and were determined to go further south next time. Just before Easter a year later we saw an advertisement in a Sunday paper which read, *PERIGORDIAN STONE COTTAGE, RIPE FOR DEVELOPMENT.* It gave a UK telephone number. I rang it. "Oh Christ! That's not still in the paper, is it?" The respondent then gave me the name and address of an estate agent in the Dordogne. It was a Monsieur Javersac who made an appointment to meet me in his office in Lalinde at 10 a.m. the following Thursday.

We duly arrived about five minutes early, and Monsieur Javersac about forty five minutes late, but as he was driving a B.M.W. and said that he had many inexpensive properties on his books which he would be happy to show us we agreed to spend the day with him. We made a note that we would like to go back to seven of the small properties we visited. The *PERIGORDIAN STONE COTTAGE* turned out to have had all wood – walls, roof timbers, floors, doors – removed, leaving a collapsing stone shell which was totally uninhabitable.

One of the small houses we revisited was in Couze. There was a little car park next to it. We stopped on the car park and a cottage door opened opposite. It was not the one we had come to see. In the doorway were a young couple who beckoned us over. The cottage was adequately equipped with electric heaters, all of which were switched on. We remembered Paris the previous year. The price was right, and we settled at once to buy. The young couple were moving to a house up the hill from the cottage as they had just had their first baby. Alas! Their marriage didn't last and the house, which we had admired, shortly came on the market. We made an offer, which was accepted, and found ourselves in possession of a four bedroom, two bathroom, charming house with an internal garage and plenty to do in the way of decorations, but completely habitable. It has been our home ever since.

As we had two dwellings in which people could sleep in comfort, it was not long before visitors began to arrive. Anne and Peter liked the look of the cottage, and agreed to pay us precisely what we had paid for it. Next door was an attached building which had been used as two workshops – the downstairs for motor cycles and the first floor for bicycles. They dextrously amalgamated the two little buildings and opened the loft for conversion to a bedroom. They now have an attractive and comfortable second home.

Anne and Peter's son Patrick was a frequent visitor to Couze and was soon on the lookout for a place of his own. Unlike Ivy and me, and Anne and Peter, who bought buildings which were immediately inhabitable, Patrick committed himself to a somewhat larger semi-detached house which required major work in both plumbing and electrics. The work has been held up by the illness of his daughter Annie, but there are signs of progress. His new appointment as European Claims Supervisor for Hertz will call on him to visit France, amongst other countries. I have confidence that with his administrative ability, he will be able to include visits to his Couze house so that he can make it possible for his family to live in it.

Another member of the family who is very fond of Couze is Ivy's son, Neil. He was a young teenager when we married. He trained as an engineer, but has since become an actor. Like most actors he has found life in this profession difficult, but he perseveres. It is what he wants to do. Neil has many friends in Couze. He comes out as often as possible, as he likes the life here. He has made a great contribution to his mother's happiness. He is the father of a very remarkable young lady named Zoe. She is alert, sensible and already at eight years old she is a very attractive young woman.

At the Villa Martine our family would be incomplete without mention of our cats Monty and Billy. Monty came to us seven and a half years ago. Debbie and Tom were visiting. It was an October evening. When we opened the door, Tom had in his hands a tiny kitten – less than three months old. The vet tells us is he is a cross between a Siamese and an ordinary grey tabby. I told Tom that we had not got a cat, and bent over to put it out. Before I could stand up again the kitten was back indoors. So we gave him some milk and the only food even roughly suitable, a little mashed up sardine. At that time the rage was for the film *The Full Monty*, so we named him Monty and have been fast friends ever since.

About a year later some misguided friend gave Danielle, the daughter of our next door neighbour, a ginger tabby kitten as a Christmas present. This was not a good idea. Danielle was going off to Bordeaux University in early January. Furthermore the Portuguese (the family come from Portugal) have little concept of animals as pets. We were aware of the little thing, probably younger than Monty had been when he adopted us, being shut out for the night – in January and February – and being fed from large tins of adult cat food. In February Adelaide went on a visit to her family in Portugal and asked us if we would feed the kitten. We agreed. We bought some suitable kitten food, brought him into a warm house, caressed him.

Editorial conference 2005

When Adelaide returned we tried to persuade the kitten to go back. The hairs stood up on his back. We were asked if we would like to keep him. We agreed, and called him Billy. Monty, although only a year older, seemed glad to adopt Billy as a younger brother. If Billy stays out late, especially in bad weather, Monty searches the house for him. We open the back door and say to Monty, "Go and find Billy". Invariably, in a very short time he comes back shepherding Billy home. For some time Billy tried to be 'top cat'. Monty was standing no nonsense, but never acted belligerently. Now they spend hours sleeping together on my bed in what is known as the boys' dormitory.

The neighbourhood round Couze is thickly wooded and was at one time the centre of the French paper-making trade. There were no less than seven major paper-making factories, of which only one now survives. In addition there is an artist's studio which specialises in the making and printing of 'art' paper.

Couze lies on the main road between Bergerac and Sarlat. From this central vantage point there are several routes in and out. Whenever we were driving together towards Bergerac our old and, alas, now deceased friend Maurice never failed to declare that there were *quatre voies*, four parallel routes going in that direction. First there was the railway. Beside it the main road. Close by the road was a canal, and beside the canal the river Dordogne. When in the nineteenth century the reciprocal traffic of raw material for the paper mills and the return rolls and bales of manufactured paper regularly passed one another, it was necessary to have as many means of transport available as possible. Hence the building of the canal to supplement the use of the river, which in any case started to flow more and more shallowly as water was taken out of it to drive a hydro-electric generation scheme.

Unlike many villages in France, Couze does not house an agricultural community. Not only was there a long history of paper making, but a new and rapidly developing factory for the manufacture of plastic piping also contributes to the industry of the village. Whilst one misses the idyllic community life which has been praised in various books about living in rural France, we have the advantages of mains electricity, central sewage collection and good roads.

France is a big country with a population about the same size as that of Great Britain. It is therefore not crowded. Main roads are good, but the innumerable side roads are well maintained and never seem excessively crowded. Central France is dotted with charming small towns like Bergerac and Sarlat and immaculate villages such as Domme (which attracts tourists, but not in such numbers as to stifle or suffocate). The Dordogne is a food growing district. Markets and shops display reasonably priced fruit and vegetables. In every village there are restaurants in which good food is on sale at very reasonable prices. The small towns are sufficiently accessible, and have enough small supermarkets and other shops to make any reasonable shopping eminently possible.

There is nothing comparable in England. I would not want to live anywhere else. Nor could I wish for better companions than my beloved wife and Monty and Billy, best of cats.

Written in Couze, France
2003 - 2005

Monty

Billy

Lightning Source UK Ltd.
Milton Keynes UK
UKHW012229270121
377782UK00002B/330